Edward Albee at Home and Abroad
A Bibliography

EDWARD ALBEE

AT HOME AND ABROAD

A Bibliography

Compiled by Richard E. Amacher
and Margaret Rule

AMS PRESS, INC · NEW YORK

Library of Congress Cataloging in Publication Data

Amacher, Richard E.
  Edward Albee at home and abroad; a bibliography.

  1. Albee, Edward, 1928–   —Bibliography.
  I. Rule, Margaret, 1913–   joint author.
II. Title.
Z8021.17.A63   016.812'5'4   73-158245
ISBN 0-404-07945-8

CONTENTS

Preface

Bibliography must always serve a utilitarian purpose. The compilers of the present bibliography have aimed at such utility by presenting a reasonably complete collection of reviews, critical articles, and miscellaneous relevant material about Edward Albee, along with his published works, to the end of facilitating research and criticism. We say "reasonably complete," because despite our attempt to track down everything in print about Albee, we found it impossible to cover exhaustively newspaper reviews outside the principle dailies in New York City, although we have included as many of such reviews as came to our attention. (Digests and other indices of drama reviews in newspapers, both here and abroad, are very scarce.) British and other foreign (except German) editions of Albee's works, we have gathered as best we could from sources such as *British Books in Print, British National Bibliography, (Biblio,)* etc. Despite these two limitations, however, we have assembled close to one thousand items, a considerable advance over previous bibliographies.

Because of Albee's great popularity in Germany, where the first production of two of his early plays occurred, we have thought it appropriate to broaden the work to include as many articles as we could find that have appeared there —and elsewhere in Europe. Thus for the first time the phenomenally large interest in Albee's plays can begin to be demonstrated. Our bibliography covers American, English, and continental material. We must add, however, that we have barely touched the less accessible data in iron-curtain countries.

Designing our work mainly for the American reader, we have not annotated the less familiar German and continental material; but we have provided descriptive notes for most of the American and English entries with the exception of reviews. Reviews of movies and books have been so

1

designated. In a few instances, we have encountered difficulty in deciding whether an item was an article or a review, and we have had to enter such items under both categories. But in general we have tried to keep such duplication (or cross reference) to an absolute minimum.

A further word of explanation about the arrangement of our material is necessary. Works written by Albee himself have been arranged in chronological order; secondary works have been arranged alphabetically; reviews have been listed in alphabetical order under the relevant plays. Foreign language articles and reviews have been grouped by country in order of the amount of critical interest thus far shown in Albee's plays. Within the specified country the order is alphabetical. While a certain degree of logical consistency may seem lost by this kind of arrangement, an undeniable gain in facility of reference results. We trust that our readers will benefit from this kind of arrangement. Our purpose has been to provide a workable tool for any reader interested in the modern American theater, its relation to the European Theater of the Absurd, and Albee's present highly controversial position with respect to both these historically important movements.

Albee has held the interest of European as well as American theater audiences and teachers for nearly a decade. (*The Zoo Story*, according to his own account written in 1958, was not produced until 1959 in Germany.) We are aware that new articles on Albee are constantly springing up and that even if we wanted, we could not possibly keep pace with them all. But we hope that our bibliography of the first decade of his works (1958 to June of 1968) will serve a useful function——for a large audience of readers here and abroad.

The German and continental parts of the bibliography were compiled by Mrs. Margaret Rule, while I collected material for the American and English sections.

Richard E. Amacher

America and England

Primary Sources
(*Arranged chronologically*)

PLAYS

(American editions)

"The Zoo Story." *Evergreen Review,* no. 12 (March–April 1960), 28–52.

The Zoo Story and The Sandbox: Two Short Plays. New York: Dramatists' Play Service, 1960. Acting edition.

The Zoo Story, The Death of Bessie Smith, The Sandbox: Three Plays, Introduced by the Author. New York: Coward-McCann, Inc., 1960.

"Fam and Yam." *Harpers Bazaar* (September 1960).

"The American Dream." *Mademoiselle* (November 1960).

The American Dream. New York: Coward-McCann, Inc. 1961.

The American Dream; The Death of Bessie Smith; Fam and Yam. New York: Dramatists' Play Service, 1962. Acting edition.

The American Dream [and] *The Zoo Story.* New York: Signet, n.d.

Two Plays by Edward Albee: The Sandbox and The Death of Bessie Smith. New York: Signet, n.d.

Who's Afraid of Virginia Woolf? New York: Atheneum, 1962.

Who's Afraid of Virginia Woolf? New York: Pocket Books, 1963–64.

The Play "The Ballad of the Sad Cafe." Carson McCullers' Novella Adapted to the Stage. Boston: Houghton Mifflin, 1963, and New York: Atheneum, 1963.

5

Tiny Alice. New York: Atheneum, 1965.

Tiny Alice. New York: Dramatists' Play Service, 1965.
Acting edition.

Tiny Alice. New York: Pocket Books, 1966.

Malcolm. New York: Atheneum, 1966.

A Delicate Balance. New York: Atheneum, 1966.

A Delicate Balance. New York: Samuel French, 1967.
Acting edition.

PLAYS

(*English editions*)

The Zoo Story and Other Plays. London: J. Cape, 1962.

Three Plays. London: H. Jonas, n.d. Capricorn Books.

The American Dream. London: S. French, [1962].

The American Dream. London: H. Jonas, n.d. Capricorn
Books.

The Death of Bessie Smith. London: S. French, [1962].

The Zoo Story. London: S. French, [1963].

Who's Afraid of Virginia Woolf? London: J. Cape, 1964.

Who's Afraid of Virginia Woolf? Harmondsworth: Penguin,
1965.

The Ballad of the Sad Cafe: the play; Carson McCullers'
Novella Adapted to the Stage. London: J. Cape, 1965.

Tiny Alice. London: J. Cape, 1966.

Malcolm: Adapted by Edward Albee from the Novel by
James Purdy. London: J. Cape with Secker and
Warburg, 1967.

A Delicate Balance. London: J. Cape, 1968.

Primary Sources

ARTICLES (AND OTHER WORKS) BY ALBEE

"What's It About?—A Playwright Tries to Tell." *New York Herald Tribune Magazine,* "The Lively Arts" (January 22, 1961), 5. Interviewed by a lady reporter from Buenos Aires, Albee talks about *The American Dream* and *Bartleby* and expresses his gratitude to the public.

"Which Theatre Is the Absurd One?" *New York Times Magazine* (February 25, 1962), 30–31, 64, 66. Defense of the Theater of the Absurd. Attacks the existing Broadway theater, which he calls the "absurd" one. Reprinted in Horst Frenz' *American Playwrights on Drama,* 168–74. Also in J. Gassner's *Directions in Modern Theater and Drama,* 329–36.

"Just What Is the Theater of the Absurd?" *Dramatists' Bulletin,* II, no. 7 (April 1962), 102. Quotes from preceding *New York Times Magazine* article.

"Some Notes on Non-Conformity." *Harper's Bazaar* (August 1962), 104. Albee lists Turgenev and Jane Austen among other non-conformists.

"Carson McCullers—the Case of the Curious Magician." *Harper's Bazaar* (January 1963), 98. Tribute to Miss McCullers.

"Novel Beginning." *Esquire,* LX (July 1963), 59–60. Excerpt from a novel in which Albee tries to fuse stream-of-consciousness technique, in style of Virginia Woolf, with stage dialogue.

"Who's Afraid of the Truth?" *New York Times,* Sunday drama section (August 18, 1963), 1.

Three Plays by Noel Coward, Introduction by Edward Albee. New York: Dell Publishing Co., 1965.

Review of Sam Shepard's play *Icarus' Mother. Village Voice* (November 25, 1965), 19.

"Who Is James Purdy?" *New York Times,* Sunday drama section (January 9, 1966), 1, 3. Discusses problems of adapting for the stage. Written on the eve of Albee's production of *Malcolm.* Pleads for wider reading of Purdy's works.

" Creativity and Commitment." *Saturday Review,* XLIX *(June 4, 1966), 26.* Short article occasioned by international P.E.N. conference in New York.

"Apartheid in the Theater." *New York Times,* Sunday drama section (July 30, 1967), 1, 6. Calls for world-wide boycott by dramatists of segregated theater audiences.

"Albee Says 'No Thanks' to John Simon." *New York Times,* Sunday drama section (September 10, 1967), 1, 8. Answers Simon's objections to award of Pulitzer prize for *A Delicate Balance.*

"The Future Belongs to Youth." *New York Times,* Sunday drama section (November 26, 1967), 1. Discussion of *Everything in the Garden,* explaining what he had done to Giles Cooper's play of this title.

Review of Lillian Ross's novel *Vertical and Horizontal. The Village Voice* (July 11, 1963), 7.

Secondary Sources
(Arranged alphabetically)

BOOKS

Adelman, Irving and Dworkin, Rita. *Modern Drama.*
Metuchen, N.J.: Scarecrow Press, 1967. P. 20–21.
Incomplete bibliography: 26 items.

Amacher, Richard E. *Edward Albee.* New York: Twayne,
1969. Analyzes plays. First two chapters present
biographical information and Albee's literary theory.

Blair, Walter, ed. Introduction to *The American Dream* in
The Literature of the United States, II, third edition.
Chicago: Scott,Foresman, 1966. Pp. 1461–1462.

Blau, Herbert. *The Impossible Theater.* New York:
Macmillan, 1964. Pp. 39–42 for discussion of Albee
and criticism of *Virginia Woolf.*

Blum, Daniel, ed. *Theatre World, 1961–62.* New York:
Chilton Co., 1962. See also same title for 1964–65.
Contains pictures, programs, and runs of season's plays.

Britannica Book of the Year (1964). Chicago: Encyclopedia
Britannica, 1964. P. 122.

Brustein, Robert. *The Theatre of Revolt: An Approach to
Modern Drama.* Boston: Little, Brown, 1964. Relates
Albee to Existential revolt and to Pirandello theme of
conflict between illusion and reality. Final chapter
deals with Artaud, Genet, and "The Theatre of
Cruelty."

——. *Seasons of Discontent.* New York: Simon and
Schuster, 1965. Repeats reviews of Albee published

9

elsewhere. Pp. 26–29; 46–49; 145–48; 155–58;
304–11.

Clurman, Harold. *The Naked Image: Observations on the
Modern Theatre.* New York: Macmillan, 1966.
Pp. 13–24 repeat reviews published elsewhere: *Zoo
Story, American Dream, Bessie Smith, Virginia Woolf,*
and *Tiny Alice.*

Cubeta, Paul M. *Modern Drama for Analysis,* third edition.
New York: Holt, Rinehart & Winston, 1962. Discern-
ing analysis of *The Sandbox.*

Debusscher, Gilbert. *Edward Albee: Tradition and Renewal.*
Brussels, Belgium: American Studies Center, 1967.
Translated by Mrs. Anne D. Williams. Oriented towards European readers and concentrates on thematic
analyses of plays. Pp. 85–94 contain a selected
bibliography.

Downer, Alan S. *The American Theater Today.* New York:
Basic Books, 1967. Pp. 111–23. Covers Albee's
biography and views of theater and movies.

Esslin, Martin. *The Theatre of the Absurd.* Garden City,
N.Y.: Doubleday, 1961. A good treatment of the
general subject. Brief discussion of *The Zoo Story,
The Death of Bessie Smith,* and *The American Dream*
and their relationship to works of Pinter and Ionesco.
Short bibliography of Albee.

Finkelstein, Sidney. *Existentialism and Alienation in
American Literature.* New York: International
Publishers, 1965. Good short analyses of *Virginia
Woolf* and *Tiny Alice.*

Flanagan, William. "Notes on the Performance of the

Musical Score for *The Sandbox.*" In *The Best Short Plays of 1959–1960.* ed. by Margaret Mayorga. Boston: Beacon Press, 1960. Pp. 69–70.

Gardner, R.H. *The Splintered Stage: The Decline of the American Theater.* New York: Macmillan, 1965. Pp. 146–153 present brief discussions of *Zoo Story, Bessie Smith, American Dream, Virginia Woolf,* and *Ballad.*

Gassner, John. *Directions in Modern Theatre and Drama.* New York: Holt, Rinehart & Winston, 1965. Contains a brief introduction to the Theater of the Absurd (pp. 326–328), and reprints Albee's article "Which Theatre Is the Absurd One?" (pp. 329–336).

Gaye, Freda, ed. *Who's Who in the Theatre,* 14th ed. New York: Pitman, 1967. P. 291.

Gould. Jean. "Edward Albee and the Current Scene." In *Modern American Playwrights.* New York: Dodd, Mead, 1966. Pp. 273-290.

Guernsey, Otis L. Jr. *The Best Plays of 1964–65.* New York: Dodd, Mead, 1965.

——. *The Best Plays of 1965–66.* New York: Dodd, Mead, 1966.

——. *The Best Plays of 1966–67.* New York: Dodd, Mead, 1967.

——. *The Best Plays of 1967–68.* New York: Dodd, Mead, 1968.

Hewes, Henry. "Off Broadway." In *The Best Plays of 1959–60,* ed. by Louis Kronenberger. New York: Dodd, Mead, 1960. Pp. 38–50.

——. "Off Broadway." In *The Best Plays of 1960–61,* ed. by Louis Kronenberger. New York: Dodd, Mead, Pp. 36–48.

——. *The Best Plays of 1961–62.* New York: Dodd, Mead, 1962.

——. *The Best Plays of 1962–63.* New York: Dodd, Mead, 1963.

——. *The Best Plays of 1963–64.* New York: Dodd, Mead, 1964.

Hilfer, Anthony C. "George and Martha: Sad, Sad, Sad." In *Seven Contemporary Authors,* ed. by T.W. Whitbread, Austin: University of Texas, 1966. Pp. 121–39. Points out Strindberg's and O'Neill's influence on content and form, respectively, in *Virginia Woolf.*

Kerr, Walter. *The Theater in Spite of Itself.* New York: Simon and Schuster, 1963. General treatment in "The Ambiguity of the Theater of the Absurd." More specific discussion of *Virginia Woolf* (pp. 122–126).

Kostelanetz, Richard. "Edward Albee." In *On Contemporary Literature.* New York: Avon, 1964. Pp. 225–231.

——."The New American Theatre." In *The New American Arts.* New York: Horizon Press, 1965. Pp. 52–62 cover *Virginia Woolf* and the shorter plays. Criticizes the one-acters for lack of unified action.

Lewis, Allan. *American Plays and Playwrights of the Contemporary Theatre.* New York: Crown Publishers, 1965. Reprints his article "The Fun and Games of Edward Albee" (pp. 81–98), but makes passing mention of Albee throughout.

Moritz, Charles, ed. *Current Biography Yearbook* (1963). New York: H.W. Wilson Co., 1963. Pp. 1–3.

Secondary Sources

Newquist, Roy. *Showcase.* New York: Morrow, 1966.
Pp. 17–29.

Reinert, Otto. *Drama, An Introductory Anthology.*
Alternate ed. Boston: Little, Brown, 1964. Pp. 866–
871, 885, and *passim* in Introduction. Criticizes *The
American Dream* and shows Albee's ties to the
absurdist movement.

Silver, Lily Jay. *Profiles In Success.* New York: Fountain-
head, 1965. Pp. 1–12.

Wager, Walter, ed. *Playwrights Speak.* New York:
Delacorte Press, 1967. Pp. 25–67.

Waith, Eugene M. *The Dramatic Moment.* Englewood
Cliffs, N.J.: Prentice-Hall, 1967. Pp. 63, 76–77,
for comment on *The Zoo Story.*

Wellworth, George. *The Theatre of Protest and Paradox.*
New York: New York University Press, 1964. Pp.
274–84 consider Albee along with other new American
dramatists.

Weales, Gerald. *American Drama Since World War II.* New
York: Harcourt, Brace & World, 1962. Brief comments
on pp. 215, 218–221, 223.

DISSERTATIONS

Dubler, Walter. *O'Neill, Wilder, and Albee: The Uses of
Fantasy in Modern American Drama.* Unpublished
Ph.D. dissertation, Harvard University, 1964.

Rule, Margaret. *Edward Albee in Germany* Unpublished
Ph.D. dissertation in progress, University of Arkansas.
Treats Albee's plays in Germany and his reputation there.

Smallwood, Clyde George. *Elements of the Existential Philosophy in "The Theatre of the Absurd"* Unpublished Ph.D. dissertation, University of Denver, 1963.

THESIS

McFarland, David T. *Intimations of Existentialism: Analogies to Religion in Three of Edward Albee's Plays* Unpublished M.A. thesis, Stetson University, 1966.

ARTICLES

Adams, Herbert R. "Albee, the Absurdists and High School English?" *English Journal,* LV (November 1966), 1045–48. Questions suitability of Albee and other absurdists for high school students and other adolescents.

"Albee." *New Yorker,* XXXVII (March 25, 1961), 30–32. Interview, containing facts of life, liking for adopted cats, modern painting, music, etc., and his work in progress at the time.

"Albee Revisited." *New Yorker,* XL (December 19, 1964), 31–33. Interview at rehearsal for *Tiny Alice.*

"Albee vs Chester." *Commentary,* XXXVI (October 1963), 272ff. Reaction to Alfred Chester's smashing attack on *Virginia Woolf* in his review (April 1963), 296–301.

"American Playwrights." *Times Literary Supplement*

(London) (June 8, 1962), 428. Brief criticism of Albee's first four plays, published in book form in England.

Armstrong, Madeleine. "Edward Albee and the American Dream." *Quadrant,* 34 (March 1965), 62–67.

"Dramatic Decline." *Times Literary Supplement* (London) (May 26, 1966), 472.

"Edward (Franklin) Albee." *Current Biography* (February 1963), 3–5. (Pp. 1–3 in bound vol.). Brief introduction to life and plays to that time—combined from six sources.

"He Can Try Anything." *Newsweek,* LXIV (May 29, 1967), 90ff.

"King of Off-Broadway." *Newsweek,* LVII (March 13, 1961), 90. Albee's success with off-Broadway productions and his work in progress. Brief criticism of *Bessie Smith.*

"Peanut Butter." *Newsweek,* LX (November 5, 1962), 74–75. Box office information on *Virginia Woolf.*

"Pulitzer Surprise: An Honor in Decline?" *National Observer* (May 8, 1967), 4.

"Talk with the Author." *Newsweek,* LX (October 29, 1962), 52–53.

"Towards a Theatre of Cruelty?" *Times Literary Supplement* (London) (February 27, 1964), 166. Excellent discussion of *The Zoo Story, Bessie Smith, The American Dream,* and *Virginia Woolf.*

"Visiting Scholar Series Extended." *Pratt Institute Quarterly News,* I, 1 (March 1963), 1.

"Who's Afraid of Success?" *Newsweek,* LXV (January 4, 1965), 51. Interview on eve of *Tiny Alice* première.

Ballew, Leighton M. "Who's Afraid of Tiny Alice?"

Georgia Review, XX (1966), 292–99. Suggests entire play takes place in Julian's mind.

Baxandall, Lee. "The Theatre of Edward Albee." *Tulane Drama Review,* IX, 4 (Summer 1965), 19-40. Freudian criticism.

Bigsby, C.W.E. "Curioser and Curioser: Edward Albee and the Great God Reality." *Modern Drama,* X (December 1967), 258–66. Finds the "symbolic pattern" is "essentially Platonic"—a revelation of "the dilemma of modern society in retreat from reality" or truth.

———. "Edward Albee's Georgia Ballad" *Twentieth Century Literature,* XIII (January 1968), 229–36. Part defense, part censure, of Albee and McCullers as writers in the Absurdist tradition.

———. *"Who's Afraid of Virginia Woolf?* Edward Albee's Morality Play" *Journal of American Studies* (October 1967), 257–68. Penetrating analysis of *Virginia Woolf* as "a modern secular morality play."

Booth, John E. "Albee and Schneider Observe: Something's Stirring." *Theatre Arts,* XLVI (March 1961), 22–24, 78–79. Interview concerning the "new" theater.

Bowers, Faubion and Loney, Glen M. "Theatre of the Absurd: It Is Only A Fad [Loney]. It Is Here To Stay [Bowers]." *Theatre Arts,* XLVI (November 1962), 20–24, 64–68. Loney writes approvingly of Albee's work; Bowers reveals insight into *The Zoo Story.*

Brody, Jane. "The Case is Familiar, but the Theater is Absurd." *New York Times* (July 15, 1967), 15. Psychiatric approach to *The Zoo Story.*

Calta, Louis. "Albee Lectures Critics on Taste." *New York Times* (March 23, 1965), 33. Report on Albee's press conference on *Tiny Alice* at Billy Rose Theater.

Cappelleti, J. "Are You Afraid of Edward Albee?" *Drama Critique,* VI (Fall 1963), 84–88. Defends Albee's rational attack on artificial values in American society.

Chabrowe, L.E. "The Pains of Being Demystified." *Kenyon Review,* XXV, 1 (1963), 142–49. Finds the Theater of the Absurd unsatisfying. Criticism of *American Dream* and *Virginia Woolf.*

Clurman, Harold. "For the Young American Playwright." *First Stage,* I, 1 (1961–62), 7–9

Cole, Douglas. "Albee's *Virginia Woolf* and Steele's *Tatler.*" *American Literature,* XL (March 1968), 81–82. Suggests a possible source for one of games in *Virginia Woolf.*

Corrigan, Robert W. "The Soulscape of American Drama." *World Theatre,* XI (Winter 1962–63), 316–28. Criticism of existential theater. Calls Albee self-conscious and imitative.

Daniel, Walter C. "Absurdity in *The Death of Bessie Smith* " *College Language Association Journal,* VIII (September 1964), 78–80. Regards the Orderly as the central character and relates his dilemma to Camus' doctrine of absurdity in *The Myth of Sisyphus.*

Davison, Richard Alan. "Edward Albee's Tiny Alice: A Note of Re-examination." *(Modern Drama,* XI (May 1968), 54–60. Interpretation of symbols in Albee's "aesthetically unified view of man' tragic struggle in an equivocal and enigmatic universe."

Deutsch, Robert H. "Writers Maturing in the Theater of the Absurd." *Discourse,* VII (Spring 1964), 181–87. Compares Albee with Ionesco. Says they present

17

same message: a world without a meaning.

Dias, Earl J. "Full-Scale Albee." *Drama Critique,* VIII (Fall 1965), 107–12. Discusses themes in *Virginia Woolf, Ballad,* and *Tiny Alice.*

Diehl, Digby. "Edward Albee Interviewed." *Transatlantic Review,* XIII (Summer 1963), 57–72. Stresses Albee's dissatisfaction with American society as a motive for his writings.

Downer, Alan S. "Love in Several Masques: Notes on the New York Theatre, 1959–1960." *Quarterly Journal of Speech,* XLVI, 3 (1960), 253–54. Discusses Off-Broadway, including *The Zoo Story.*

Driver, Tom F. "What's the Matter with Edward Albee?" *Reporter,* XXX (January 2, 1964), 38–39. Caustic analysis of Albee's failure to maintain realistic conventions of theater and identification of him with "the dream" of the bourgeois theater. Reprinted in A.S. Downer's *American Drama and Its Critics,* pp. 240–44. [See pp. 10, 12, of January 30, 1964 issue for three letters in response to Driver's article.]

DuKore, Bernard F. "Tiny Albee." *Drama Survey,* V (Spring 1966), 60–66. Regards play as symbolic but obscure.

——."A Warp in Albee's *Woolf." Southern Speech Journal,* XXX (Winter 1964), 261–68. Compares *Virginia Woolf* with *Medea.*

Evans, Arthur. "Love, History and Albee." *Renascence,* XVIII (Spring 1967), 115–18, 131. Sees characters in *Virginia Woolf* trapped but trying to free themselves by divine love.

Ferguson, Francis R. "A Conversation with Digby R. Diehl." *Transatlantic Review* (Spring 1965), 115–21.

Criticizes *Virginia Woolf* as narrow, unsophisticated, and unrelated to our time.

Filandro, Anthony and Dolores. Letter to editor, *Commentary,* XXXVI, 4 (1963), 272–73. Relates *Virginia Woolf* to Jason and Medea story.

Finkelstein, Sidney. "Norman Mailer and Edward Albee." *American Dialog,* II (February–March 1965), 23–28. Compares different brands of existentialism in the two writers.

Flanagan, William. "Albee in the Village." *New York Herald Tribune* (October 27, 1963), 27. Impressions of Albee by a friend who roomed with him for nine years.

——."The Art of the Theater IV: Edward Albee, An Interview." *Paris Review,* X (Fall 1966), 92–121.

—— .[No title] *American Composers Alliance Bulletin,* IX, 4 (1961), 12–13.

Flasch, Mrs. Harold A. "Games People Play in *"Who's Afraid of Virginia Woolf."Modern Drama,* X (December 1967), 280–88. Uses Eric Berne's *Games People Play* as key to games in *Virginia Woolf.*

Franzblau, Abraham N. "A Psychiatrist Looks at 'Tiny Alice,' " *Saturday Review,* XLVIII (January 30, 1965), 39. Speculations on meaning of the play.

Gardner, Paul. " 'Tiny Alice' Mystifies Albee, Too." *New York Times* (January 21, 1965), 22. Interview.

Gelb, Arthur. "Dramatists Deny Nihilistic Trend." *New York Times* (February 15, 1960), 23. Interviews with Albee and Gelber.

Gilman, Richard. "The Drama Is Coming Now." *Tulane Drama Review,*VII (Summer 1963), 27–42. Gilman sees Albee continuing American tradition rather than "more meaningful" tradition of European theater.

G[ingrich], A[rnold]. "Publisher's Page:A Lively and Responsive Weekend at Princeton." *Esquire,* LX (July 1963), 111–12. Report on Albee's participation in the seminars devoted to excellence in the fine arts, which attracted students from fifty colleges besides Princeton.

Goodman, Henry. "The New Dramatists: 4. Edward Albee." *Drama Survey,* II (1962), 72–79. Says Albee's plays are "ferocious attacks" on American society and its false values.

Goodman, Randolph. "Playwatching with a Third Eye: Fun and Games with Albee, Ibsen, and Strindberg." *Columbia University Forum,* X (Spring 1967), 18–22. Parallels between *Virginia Woolf* and *Hedda Gabler.* Says Ibsen purportedly based the latter play on Strindberg's life.

Grande, Luke M. "Edward Albee's 'Bessie Smith': Alienation/the Color-Problem." *Drama Critique,* V (May 1962), 66–69. Sees man's alienation from man as more important than racial alienation in this play.

Gray, Wallace. "The Uses of Incongruity." *Educational Theatre Journal,* XV (December 1963), 343–47. Albee's use of incongruity as an important technique in modern drama.

Gussow, Mel. "Albee, Odd Man In On Broadway." *Newsweek,* LXI (February 4, 1963), 49–52. Interview, with several pictures of Albee and his mother, Frances Albee. Relates him to other young American dramatists: Gelber, Richardson, Kopit.

Hamilton, Kenneth. "Mr. Albee's Dream." *Queen's Quarterly,* LXX (Autumn 1963), 393–99. Regards

Albee's social criticism as superficial.

Harris, Wendell. "Morality, Absurdity, and Albee."
Southwest Review, XLIX (1964), 249–256.

Hewes, Henry. "The Tiny Alice Caper." *Saturday Review,*
XLVIII (January 30, 1965), 38, 39, 65. Digest of
Tiny Alice criticism along with interviews with Albee,
Gielgud, Irene Worth, and Alan Schneider.

——"Upon Your Imaginary Forces, ACT!" *Saturday
Review,* XLVIII (September 4, 1965), 43. Report on
William Ball's production of *Tiny Alice* at the
Pittsburgh American Conservatory Theatre.

Hill, Carol D. "Edward Albee." Letter to editor.
Massachusetts Review, VI, 3 (1965), 649–50. Affirms
position of Charles T. Samuels. See infra.

Irwin, Ray. "Who's Afraid of Virginia Woolf, Hunh?"
Atlantic Monthly, CCXIII (April 1964), 122–124.
Spoof of close textual study but also a criticism of
Albee's diction. Found the word *Hunh* used fifty-five
times during the play. Says "Mr. Albee clearly has
something in mind."

Jamieson, Daniel J. "On Edward Albee." *Teachers College
Record,* LXVIII (January 1967), 352–53. Considers
problem of truth vs illusion in *American Dream,
Virginia Woolf, Tiny Alice, A Delicate Balance.*

Jennings, Robert. "Playboy Interview: Mike Nichols."
Playboy, XIII (June 1966), 63ff. Interview.

Johnson, Carolyn E. "In Defense of Albee." *English
Journal* (January 1968), 21–23. Considers *Virginia
Woolf* and *Zoo Story* for high school students.

Kihss, Peter. "Albee Wins Pulitzer Prize." *New York Times*
(May 2, 1967), 1.

Kleiner, Dick. "Young-Old Albee Finds Success with

Off-Broadway One-Actors," *New York World Telegram & Sun* (May 20, 1961).

Knepler, Henry. "Conflict of Traditions in Edward Albee." *Modern Drama,* X (December 1967), 274–79. Sees Albee thus far trapped between two irreconcilable traditions—American and European Absurdist.

Kosner, Edward. "Social Critics, Like Prophets, Are Often Honored from Afar." *New York Post* (March 31, 1961), 38. Interview with pictures.

Kostelanetz, Richard. "The Art of Total No." *Contact,* 16 (October–November 1963), 62–70.

La Fontane, Barbara, "Triple Threat On, Off and Off-Off Broadway." *New York Times* (February 25, 1968), 36–37, 39, 40, 42, 44, 46. Well-written, important article on Albee as person. Also treats Albee-Barr-Wilder producing agency and their encouragement to young dramatists.

Lahr, John. "Theater: a question long overdue." *Arts Magazine,* XLI (May 1967), 21–23. Compares Albee unfavorably with Beckett and Pinter.

——."The Adaptable Mr. Albee." *Evergreen Review* (May 1968), 37–39, 82–87. Criticism of Albee's adaptations — *Malcolm, Ballad,* and *Everything in the Garden.*

Lewis, Allan. "The Fun and Games of Edward Albee." *Educational Theatre Journal,* XVI (March 1964), 29–39. Good criticism of *The Zoo Story* and *Virginia Woolf.* Less penetrating on other Albee plays. [Reprinted in *American Plays and Playwrights of Contemporary Theatre,* 81–98.]

Lipton, Edward. "The *Tiny Alice* Enigma." *Saturday Review,* XLVIII (February 20, 1965), 21. Letter to editor from an M.D. Offers insight to important problems in the play by use of psychoanalytic approach to the character of Julian.

Lukas, Mary. "Who Isn't Afraid of Edward Albee?" *Show* (February 1963), 83, 112–14. Interview on occasion of *Virginia Woolf.* Contains much biographical material with psychological theories about Albee's early life and its effect on his artistic temperament.

Lyons, Charles R. "On the Zoo Story." *Drama Survey,* IV (Summer 1965), 121–37.

——."Some Variations of 'Kindermord' as Dramatic Archetype." *Comparative Drama,* I (Spring 1967), 56–71. Discusses *Virginia Woolf* among other plays.

——."Two Projections of the Isolation of the Human Soul: Brecht's *Im Dickicht der Staedte* and Albee's *The Zoo Story.*" *Drama Survey,* IV (Summer 1965), 121–138.

Markus, Thomas B. *"Tiny Alice and Tragic Catharsis."* *Educational Theatre Journal,* XVII (October 1965), 225–233.

McDonald, Daniel. "Truth and Illusion in *Who's Afraid of Virginia Woolf?*" *Renascence,* XVII (Winter 1964), 63–69.

Meehan, Thomas. "Edward Albee and a Mystery." *New York Times,* Sunday drama section (December 27, 1964), 1, 16. Interview with author on eve of *Tiny Alice* première.

Merritt, Robert. "Exploding Time and Space." *Tulane Drama Review,* IX (Winter 1964), 182–90. Interview with first director of *The Zoo Story.*

Miller, Jordan Y. "Myth and the American Dream: O'Neill to Albee." *Modern Drama,* VII (1964), 190–198.

Compares Albee's handling of this subject in *American Dream* with that of William's *Camino Real* and O'Neill's *The Great God Brown.*

Morgan, Thomas B. "Angry Playwright in a Soft Spell." *Life* (May 26, 1967), 90–99. Recent interview with pictures and biographical information.

Mottram, Eric. "The New American Wave." *Encore Magazine,* XI (January-February 1964), 22–41. Discusses Albee along with others in this movement.

Newman, David. "Four Make a Wave." *Esquire,* LV (April 1961), 45–51. The American Theater of the Absurd Albee, Gelber, Richardson, and Kopit—with a review of *The Zoo Story.*

Oberg, Arthur K. "Edward Albee: His Language and Imagination." *Prairie Schooner,* XL (1966), 139–146.

"Off-Broadway." *Newsweek,* LVII (March 13, 1961), 91. Cost and profit of *The Zoo Story.*

Peck, Seymour. "Williams and 'The Iguana.' " *New York Times* (December 24, 1961), 5. This interview with Williams gives some of his remarks on Albee.

Phillips, Elizabeth C. "Albee and the Theatre of the Absurd." *Tennessee Studies in Literature,* X (1965), 73–80. Uses Albee's plays to illustrate Esslin's list of techniques employed by British and European absurdists: difficulty of communication (*The Zoo Story*); absence of plot (*Bessie Smith*); deterioration of language (*The Sandbox*); "horror pervading and permeating the comic" (*The American Dream*); and symbolism projecting "man's deepest fears and anxieties" (*Virginia Woolf*).

Plotinsky, M.L. "Transformation of Understanding: Edward Albee in the Theatre of the Irresolute."

Drama Survey, IV (Winter 1965), 220–32.

Raymont, Henry. "Campaign by Artists." *New York Times* (July 14, 1967), 9. Includes text of Albee's letter to Isaac Stern, urging boycott of summer music festival in Athens, in order to protest loss of citizenship of Miss Melina Mercouri.

Robertson, Roderick. "A Theatre for the Absurd: The Passionate Equation." *Drama Survey,* II, 1 (1962), 24–43.

Roy, Emil. "Who's Afraid of Virginia Woolf? and the Tradition." *Bucknell Review,* XIII (March 1965), 27–36. Points out similarities in technique between *Virginia Woolf* and earlier works of Naturalistic, Realistic, and Existentialist traditions. Analysis of the plot.

Rule, Margaret W. "An Edward Albee Bibliography." *Twentieth Century Literature* (April 1968), 35–45. Best bibliography to date.

Samuels, Charles T. "The Theatre of Edward Albee." *Massachusetts Review,* VI (Autumn 1964), 187–201. See Hill, C.D. in (Spring 1965), 649–650, for congratulations and for agreement.

Schechner, Richard. "Reality Is Not Enough: An Interview with Alan Schneider." *Tulane Drama Review,* IX, 3 (1965), 118–52. [Schneider has directed nearly all of Albee's plays.]

Schier, Donald. "Who Cares Who's Afraid of Virginia Woolf?" *Carleton Miscellany,* V, 2 (1964), 121–24.

Schneider, Alan. "Why So Afraid?" *Tulane Drama Review,* VII, 3 (Spring 1963), 10–13. Defense of *Virginia Woolf* by its director against the attack of Richard Schechner in same issue, pp. 7–10.

Siegel, Paul N. "The Drama and the Thwarted American
    Dream." *Lock Haven Review,* 7 (1965), 52–62.
    Discusses Albee's *American Dream* among plays by
    others.
Simon, John. "Should Albee Have Said 'No Thanks'?"
    New York Times (August 20, 1967), 1.
"Sketches of Winners of Pulitzer Prizes." *New York Times*
    (May 2, 1967), 40.
Skow, John. "Broadway's Hottest Playwright, Edward
    Albee." *Saturday Evening Post,* CCXXXVII (January
    18, 1964), 32–33. Interview with pictures. Several
    erratic statements. Shows growth of Albee's
    reputation.
Smith, Michael. "Edward Albee in Conversation with
    Michael Smith." *Plays and Players* (March 1964),
    12–14. Interview in England.
Spencer, Sharon D. "Edward Albee—the Anger Artist."
    Forum (Texas) IV (Winter-Spring 1967), 25–30.
    Thinks Albee is related to the "sick" comics in
    revealing widespread anxiety, frustration, and delusion.
Spielberg, Peter. "The Albatross in Albee's Zoo." *College
    English,* XXVII (April 1966), 562–565. Brilliant
    example of fallacious reasoning, arguing analogically
    for "The Rime of the Ancient Mariner" as the
    principal literary source of *The Zoo Story.* See
    (October 1966), 58–59, for reaction to this article.
Stewart, R.S. "John Gielgud and Edward Albee Talk
    About the Theater." *Atlantic Monthly,* CCXV
    (April 1965), 61–68. Interviews in connection with
    Tiny Alice. Presents Albee's theories of writing and
    the responsibilities of modern playwrights.
Sullivan, Dan. "Albee Criticizes Pulitzer Board." *New*

York Times (May 3, 1967), 49.

—— ."Albee's Home Is Setting for a First Rehearsal."
New York Times (October 24, 1967), 50. Concerns
Everything in the Garden.

Times Literary Supplement (London) (January 6, 1966),
13. Notice of British edition of *Ballad.*

Tallmer, Jerry. "Edward Albee, Playwright." *New York
Post,* Sunday magazine section (November 4, 1962),
10. Interview.

—— ."Hold That Tiger." *Evergreen Review,* XVIII (May-
June 1961), 109—13.

Taylor, Marion A. "Edward Albee and August Strindberg:
Some Parallels Between the *Dance of Death* and
Who's Afraid of Virginia Woolf?" *Papers on English
Language and Literature,* I, 1 (1965), 59—71. See,
also, further note in II, 2 (1966), 187—88.

Trilling, Diana. "Who's Afraid of the Culture Elite?"
Esquire, LX (December 1963), 69ff. Wordy and at
times digressive attack on Albee as encouraging (or
holding out) the undemocratic process of member-
ship in an exclusive club to his audiences. Contains
some good criticism of Existentialist philosophy, as
well as of modern literature and life; but it is marred
with several bad generalizations.

Turner, W.L. "Absurdist, Go Home!" *Players Magazine,*
XL (February 1964), 139—40. Reaction against
influence of European theater and a plea for a more
American theater.

Valgemae, Mardi. "Albee's Great God Alice." *Modern
Drama,* X (December 1967), 267—77. Compares
Tiny Alice with O'Neill's *The Great God Brown.*

Watts, Richard, Jr. "The High Talent of Edward Albee."

New York Post (February 5, 1961). Appreciative criticism of Albee's gifts.

Weales, Gerald. "Off-Broadway: Its Contribution to American Drama." *Drama Survey,* II, 1 (1962), 5–23.

Weatherby, W.J. "Do You Like Cats?" *Manchester Guardian* (June 19, 1962), 7. Interview with pictures.

Wellwarth, George E. "Hope Deferred: The New American Drama. Reflections on Edward Albee, Jack Richardson, Jack Gelber, and Arthur Kopit." *Literary Review,* VII (Autumn 1963), 7–26. Discussion of *The Zoo Story, Bessie Smith, American Dream,* and *Virginia Woolf,* 8–15.

Wetzsteon, Ross. "Albee Pulls Surprise." *The Village Voice* (May 4, 1967), 1. On Albee's acceptance of Pulitzer prize.

Witherington, Paul. "Language of Movement in Albee's *The Death of Bessie Smith.*" *Twentieth Century Literature,* XIII (July 1967), 84–88. Sees "conflict between intention and performance" as key to this play. Approach is limited to imagery, diction, and an abstract thesis of "stasis and misdirected action."

Wolfe, Peter. "The Social Theatre of Edward Albee." *Prairie Schooner,* XXXIX (Fall 1965), 248–262. Examines eight Albee plays for social criticism.

Zimbardo, Rose A. "Symbolism and Naturalism in Edward Albee's *The Zoo Story.*" *Twentieth Century Literature,* VIII (April 1962), 10–17. Points out use of Christian and classical myth and symbolism.

Zindel, Paul and Yerby, Loree. "Interview with Edward Albee." *Wagner* [College] *Literary Magazine,* 3 (1962), 1–10.

Zolotow, Sam. "New Albee Play Fills Chief Role." *New*

Secondary Sources

York Times (October 21, 1965), 56. Casting and
advance information about *Malcolm.*
——. "Producing Team Plans Repertory." *New York
Times* (September 5, 1967), 50. Albee, Barr, and Wilder's
plans for revival of short plays by Albee, Le Roi
Jones, and Pinter along with two new one-act plays
by Albee: *"Box* and *Quotations   from Chairman Mao
Tse-tung."*

REVIEWS

Salem, James M. *A Guide to Critical Reviews.* New York:
    Scarecrow Press, 1966. Volume I, pp. 9–11, includes
    a list of reviews and other relevant material from
    periodicals and two newspaper sources: the *New
    York Times* and the *New York Theatre Critics'
    Reviews.* Covers period January, 1960, to July, 1965.

The Zoo Story

"Albee Double Bill Is Praised in Paris." *New York Times*
    (February 13, 1965), 10.
Atkinson, Brooks. "Theatre: A double Bill off Broadway."
    New York Times (January 15, 1960), 37.
——:"Village Vagrants." *New York Times* (January 31,
    1960), section II, 1.
Brustein, Robert. "Krapp and a Little Claptrap." *New
    Republic,* CXLII (February 22, 1960), 21–22.
Calta, Louis. "Beckett and Albee Back in Double Bill."
    New York Times (June 9, 1965), 42.
Clurman, Harold. "Theatre." *Nation,* CXC (February 13,
    1960), 153–54.

Driver, Tom F. "Drama: Bucketful of Dregs." *Christian Century,* LXXVII (1960), 193—94.

Funke, Lewis. "Theater: Albee Revivals." *New York Times* (May 29, 1963), 39.

Hewes, Henry. "Benchmanship." *Saturday Review,*XLIII (February 6, 1960), 32.

Lenoir, Jean-Pierre. "Two Plays by Albee Offered in Paris." *New York Times* (June 11, 1963), 29.

Lester, Bill. "This Property Is Condemned and The Zoo Story." *Plays and Players,* (October 1960), 13.

Lewis, Theophilus. "Theatre." *America: National Catholic Weekly,* CVIII (June 22, 1963), 891—892. Also covers *American Dream.*

Malcolm, Donald. "Off-Broadway." *New Yorker,* XXXV (January 23, 1960), 75—76.

Newman, David. "Four Make a Wave." *Esquire,* LV (April 1961), 48—50.

Richards, Stanley. "On and Off Broadway." *Players Magazine,* XXXVII (October 1960), 10.

Sheed, Wilfred. "Back to the Zoo." *Commonweal,* LXXXII (July 9, 1965), 501—02.

"U.S. Play Bows at Berlin Fete." *New York Times* (September 29, 1959), 45.

" 'Zoo Story' in London." *New York Times* (August 26, 1960), 13.

The Sandbox

Gelb, Arthur. " '4 in 1' Bill of One-Act Plays Opens at the Jazz Gallery." *New York Times* (May 17, 1960), 42.

West, Anthony. "The Subhuman Theatre." *Show* (July 1962), 27.

Secondary Sources

The Death of Bessie Smith

"Albee's Double Bill Is Staged in London." *New York Times* (October 25, 1961), 33.

Balliett, Whitney. "Empress of the Blues." *New Yorker,* XXXVII (March 11, 1961), 114. Also reviews *The American Dream.*

Brustein, Robert. "Fragments from a Cultural Explosion." *New Republic,* CXLIV (March 27, 1961), 29–30. Also reviews *The American Dream.*

Clurman, Harold. "Theatre." *Nation,* CXCII (March 18, 1961), 242.

Gellert, Roger. "Albee et al." *New Statesman,* LXII (November 3, 1961), 667–68. Also reviews *The American Dream.*

Grande, Luke M. "Edward Albee's Bessie Smith Alienation —the Color Problem." *Drama Critique,* V (May 1962), 66–69.

Hatch, Robert. "Arise Ye Playgoers of the World." *Horizon,* III (July 1961), 116–17. Also reviews *The American Dream.*

Hayes, Richard. "At the Albee." *Commonweal,* LIV (August 25, 1961), 471–72.

Lenoire, Jean-Pierre. "Two Plays Offered by Albee in Paris." *New York Times* (June 11, 1963), 29.

Lukas, Mary. *"The Death of Bessie Smith* and *The American Dream." Catholic World,* CXCIII (August 1961), 335–36.

Pryce-Jones, Alan. "Alan Pryce-Jones at the Theatre." *Theatre Arts,* XLV (May 1961), 56. Also reviews *The American Dream.*

Taubman, Howard. "Theatre: Intense Hour." *New York*

Times (March 2, 1961), 19.

Fam and Yam

Gelb, Arthur. "Theatre: Three One-Acters." *New York Times* (October 26, 1960), 44.

The American Dream

"Albee Double Bill Is Praised in Paris." *New York Times* (February 13, 1965), 10.

"Albee's Double Bill Is Staged in London." *New York Times* (October 25, 1961), 33.

Balliett, Whitney. "Three Cheers for Albee." *New Yorker,* XXXVI (February 4, 1961), 62, 64–66.

Brustein, Robert. "Fragments from a Cultural Explosion." *New Republic,* CXLIV (March 27, 1961), 30. Also reviews *Bessie Smith.*

Clurman, Harold. "Theatre." *Nation,* CXCII (February 11, 1961), 125–26.

Driver, Tom. "A Milestone and a Fumble." *Christian Century,* LXXVIII (March 1, 1961), 275.

"Farce from Ionesco." *Time,* LXXVII (February 3, 1961), 55.

Funke, Lewis. "Theatre: Albee Revivals." *New York Times* (May 29, 1963), 39.

Gassner, John. "Broadway in Review." *Educational Theatre Journal,* XIII (May 1961), 109–10.

Gellert, Roger. "Albee et al." *New Statesman,* LXII (November 3, 1961), 667–68. Also reviews *Bessie Smith.*

Hatch, Robert. "Arise Ye Playgoers of the World." *Horizon,* III (July 1961), 116–17. Also reviews *Bessie Smith.*

Hewes, Henry. "On Our Bad Behaviour." *Saturday Review,*
XLIV (February 11, 1961), 54.

Lewis, Theophilus. *"The Zoo Story* and *The American
Dream."America,* CVIII (June 22, 1963), 891–92.

Lukas, Mary. *"The Death of Bessie Smith* and *The American
American Dream." Catholic World,* CXCIII (August
1961), 335–36.

Popkin, Henry. "Theatre Chronicle." *Sewanee Review,*
LXIX (1961), 342–43.

Pryce-Jones, Alan. "Alan Pryce-Jones at the Theatre."
Theatre Arts, XLV (March 1961), 68.

"Sydney Offering a Lunch Theatre." *New Tork Times*
(October 20, 1963), 72.

Taubman, Howard. "The Theatre: Albee's 'The American
Dream.' " *New York Times* (January 25, 1961), 28.

"Theater: The Un-Angry." *Time,* LXXVII (February 3,
1961), 53, 55.

Trotta, G. "On Stage: Edward Albee." *Horizon,* IV
(September 1961), 79.

Who's Afraid of Virginia Woolf?

"Albee Play Divides Stockholm Critics." *New York Times*
(Octboer 6, 1963), 68.

"Blood Sport." *Time,* LXXX (October 26, 1962), 84–86.

Brustein, Robert. "Albee and the Medusa Head." *New
Republic,* CXLVII (November 3, 1962), 29–30.

Callenbach, E. "Who's Afraid of Virginia Woolf?" *Film
Quarterly,* XX, 1 (1966), 45–48.

Chester, Alfred. "Edward Albee: Red Herrings and
White Whales." *Commentary,* XXXV (April 1963),
296–301. See also, October, 1963 issue,pp. 272–75

for reaction to this review.

Chiaromonte, Nicolo. "Who's Afraid of Virginia Woolf?" *New York Review of Books,* I, 1 (1963), 16.

Clurman, Harold. "Theatre." *Nation,* CXCV (October 27, 1962), 273–74.

Coleman, D.C. "Fun and Games: Two Pictures of *Heartbreak House.*" *Drama Survey,* V (Winter 1966–67), 223–36.

Duprey, Richard A. "Who's Afraid of Virginia Woolf?" *Catholic World,* CXCVI (January 1963), 263–64.

"Edward Albee on a Love-Hate Marriage." London *Times* (November 5, 1962), 14.

Fruchter, Norm. "Albee's Broadway Break-Thru." *Encore Magazine,* X (January-February 1963), 44–48.

Galbraith, John Kenneth. "The Mystique of Failure: A Latter-Day Reflection on 'Who's Afraid of Virginia Woolf?' " *Show* (May 1964), 112.

"Game of Truth." *Newsweek,* LX (October 29, 1962), 52.

Gassner, John. "Broadway in Review." *Educational Theatre Journal,* XV (March 1963), 77–80.

— —." 'Who's Afraid of Virginia Woolf?' on LP." *Saturday Review,* XLVI (June 29, 1963), 39–40.

Gellert, Roger. "Sex-War Spectacular." *New Statesman,* LXVII (February 14, 1964), 262.

Gilman, Richard. "Here We Go Round the Albee Bush." *Commonweal,* LXXVII (November 9, 1962), 175–76.

Hewes, Henry. "Bravo Belgrade." *Saturday Review,* LI (July 20, 1968), 35. Review of Belgrade's Atelje 212 production at Lincoln Center.

— —."Who's Afraid of Big Bad Broadway?" *Saturday Review,* XLV (October 27, 1962), 29.

Hughes, C. "Edward Albee: Who's Afraid of What?"

Critic, XXI (March 1963), 16–19.

Lewis, Allan. "The Fun and Games of Edward Albee." *Educational Theatre Journal,* XVI (March 1964), 29–39.

Lewis, Theophilus. "Who's Afraid of Virginia Woolf?" *America,* CVII (November 17, 1962), 1105–06.

"London Acclaims 'Virginia Woolf.' " *New York Times* (February 8, 1964), 15.

McCarten, John. "Long Night's Journey into Daze." *New Yorker,* XXXVIII (October 20, 1962), 85–86.

Mannes, Marya. "The Half-World of American Drama." *Reporter,* XXVIII (April 25, 1963), 48–50.

Marowitz, Charles. "Who's Afraid of Virginia Woolf?" *Encore Magazine,* XI, 2 (1964), 51–52.

New York Theatre Critics Reviews, XXIII, 17 (October 22, 1962), 251–54, for newspaper reviews by John Chapman, Robert Coleman, Walter Kerr, John McClain, Norman Nadel, Howard Taubman, and Richard Watts Jr. See also, John McClain's "Two Faces of Mr. Albee" in *New York Journal American,* October 21, 1962.

"Openings, New York." *Theatre Arts,* XLVI (November 1962), 10–11.

"People Are Talking About Edward Albee." *Vogue,* CXL (December 1962), 120–21.

Potter, Stephen. "Who's Afraid of Virginia Woolf? Not Columbia." *American Record Guide,* XXIX (August 1963), 924–927.

Prideaux, Tom. "The Albee Attitude, Both Sweet and Sour." *Life,* LIII (December 14, 1962), 110.

Pryce-Jones, David. "The Rules of the Game." *Spectator,* CCXII (February 14, 1964), 213–14.

Richards, Stanley. "Theatre in New York." *Players Magazine,* XXXIX (December 1962), 85.

Robinson, Leonard Wallace. "A Bunch of Drunks." *Jubilee,* X (February 1963), 55.

"Run in Tokyo Ends for 'Virginia Woolf.' " *New York Times* (November 26, 1964), 52.

Schechner, Richard. "Who's Afraid of Edward Albee?" *Tulane Drama Review,* VII (Spring 1963), 7–10.

Silver, Margery. Letter to editor. *Commentary,* XXXVI, 4 (1963), 272.

Simon, John. "On Broadway and Off." *Harper's Magazine,* CCXXVI (March 1963), 272.

——"Theatre Chronicle." *Hudson Review,* XV (Winter 1962–63), 571–73.

"A Surprising Liz in a Film Shocker." *Life,* LX (June 10, 1966), 87–91. Review of the movie.

Taubman, Howard. "Cure for the Blues." *New York Times* (October 28, 1962), section II, 1.

Thompson, Thomas. "Raw Dialogue Challenges All the Censors." *Life,* LX (June 10, 1966), 92, 96–98. Review of the movie.

Trewin, J.C. "Nights with the Ripsaw." *Illustrated London News,* CCXLIV (February 22, 1964), 288.

" 'Virginia Woolf' in Rome." *New York Times* (November 9, 1963), 15.

Von Dreele, W.H. "The Twentieth Century and All That." *National Review,* XIV (January 15, 1963), 35–36.

Weatherby, W.J. "Albee on Broadway." *Manchester Guardian* (October 15, 1962), 7.

"Who's Afraid of Virginia Woolf?" *Listener,* LXXI (February 20, 1964), 313.

World Premières, XIV (January 1963), 60.

Secondary Sources

The Ballad of the Sad Cafe

Brustein, Robert. "The Playwight as Impersonator." *New Republic,* CXLIX (November 16, 1963), 28–29.

Clurman, Harold. "Theatre." *Nation,* CXCVII (November 23, 1963), 353–54.

Gilman, Richard. "Albee's Sad Ballad." *Commonweal,* LXXIX (November 22, 1963), 256–57.

Hall, J. *Books and Bookmen,* XI (November 1965), 459. Review of the book.

Hardwick, Elizabeth. "Theatre." *Vogue,* CXLIII (January 1, 1964), 20.

Hewes, Henry. "Dismemberment of the Wedding." *Saturday Review,* XLVI (November 16, 1963), 54.

Kostelanetz, Richard. "Albee's Sad Cafe." *Sewanee Review,* LXXII, 4 (1964), 724–26. Belated review (listed under *drama* rather than under books in index). Considers Albee's failure to adapt well.

Lewis, Theophilus. "Theatre." *America,* CX (January 4, 1964), 26.

"Lonesome Lovers." *Time,* LXXXII (November 8, 1963), 67.

McCarten, John. "Tormented Trio." *New Yorker,* XXXIX (November 9, 1963), 95.

Morse, Ben. "Three Ballads." *Players Magazine,* XL, 5 (1964), 138.

New York Theatre Critics Reviews, XXIV, 16 (1963), 212–16. Contains newspaper reviews by John Chapman, Walter Kerr, John McClain, Norman Nadel, Howard Taubman, and Richard Watts Jr.

Simon, John. "Theatre Chronicle." *Hudson Review,* XVII (Spring 1964), 81–83.

Sontag, Susan. "Going to the Theater." *Partisan Review,*
    XXXI (Winter 1964), 97–98.

Taubman, Howard. "Nature of Love." *New York Times*
    (November 10, 1963), section II, 1.

"Too Too Solid Flesh." *Newsweek,* LXII (November 11,
    1963), 76.

Ulanov, Barry. "Brecht and Albee." *Catholic World,*
    CXCVIII (January 1964), 263–64.

Von Dreele, W.H. "A Master Carpenter." *National Review,*
    XVI (January 14, 1964), 34–35.

Tiny Alice

"A Tale Within a Tail." *Time,* LXXXV (January 15, 1965),
    68, 70.

"Albee Play Puzzles New York." London *Times* (January
    7, 1965), 7.

Bannon, B.A. *Publishers' Weekly,* CLXXXIX (February 21,
    1966), 195. Review of book.

Brustein, Robert. "Three Plays and a Protest." *New
    Republic,* CLII (January 23, 1965), 32–36.

Cavenaugh, Arthur. "Tiny Alice." *Sign,* XLIV (March
    1965), 27.

Chapman, John. "Edward Albee's 'Tiny Alice,' or The
    Temptation of John Gielgud." *New York Daily News*
    (December 30, 1964). In *New York Theatre Critic's
    Reviews,* XXV (1964), 97.

"Chinese Boxes." *Newsweek,* LXV (January 11, 1965), 75.

Choice: Books for College Libraries, II (July-August 1965),
    309.

Clurman, Harold. "Tiny Alice; Hughie." *Nation,* CC
    (January 18, 1965), 65.

Secondary Sources

Dundy, Elaine. "What Means Tiny Alice?" *New York Herald Tribune* (January 31, 1965), 16, 17, 27. Gives reactions of various persons to meaning or lack of meaning in *Tiny Alice*.

Freedley, George. *Library Journal,* XC (March 15, 1965), 1343. Review of book.

Hewes,Henry. "Through the Looking Glass, Darkly." *Saturday Review,* XLVIII (January 16, 1965), 40.

——:"The Tiny Alice Caper." *Saturday Review,* XLVII (January 30, 1965), 38–39, 65.

——:"Upon Your Imaginary Forces ACT!" *Saturday Review,* XLVIII (September 4, 1965), 43.

Kelly, Kevin. Review of New York production. *The Boston Globe,* (December 30, 1964), 8.

Lerner, Max. "Who's Afraid of Edward Albee?" *New York Post* (February 3, 1965). Available in newspaper branch of New York Public Library.

Lewis, Theophilus. "Tiny Alice." *America,* CXII (March 6, 1965), 336–37.

Lipton, Edward. "The Tiny Alice Enigma." *Saturday Review,* XLVIII (February 20, 1965), 21.

Little, Stuart. "Albee Talks – but Doesn't Tell Meaning of 'Tiny Alice'." *New York Herald Tribune* (January 20, 1965), 16.

Loney, Glenn M. "Broadway in Review." *Educational Theatre Journal,* XVII (March 1965), 66–67.

Markson, John W. "Tiny Alice: Edward Albee's Negative Oedipal Enigma." *American Image,* XXIII (1966), 3–21.

Martin, Paulette. "A Theatre of Mystery." *Commonweal,* LXXXIV (September 16, 1966), 582–85.

McCarten, John. "Mystical Manipulations." *New Yorker,*

XL (January 9, 1965), 84.

McKinnon, George. Review of Boston revival. *The Boston Globe* (January 3, 1967), 18.

Muggeridge, Malcolm. "Books." *Esquire,* LXIII (April 1965), 58, 60.

New York Theatre Critics' Reviews, XXV (1964), 95–98. Newspaper reviews by Norman Nadel, Howard Taubman, John McClain, John Chapman, Richard Watts Jr.,and Walter Kerr. For further comment by Kerr, see *New York Herald Tribune* (January 17, 1965), 25, and (January 24, 1965), 24.

Popkin, Henry. "Theatre: *Tiny Alice,* 'preposterous lack of proportion.' " *Vogue,* CXLV (February 15, 1965), 50.

Prideaux, Tom. "Who Needs Answers for Albee?" *Life,* LVIII (January 29, 1965), 14.

Pumphrey, Byron. "Theater." *Arts and Architecture,* LXXXIII (April 1966), 34–35. Review of Los Angeles production.

Rogoff, Gordon. "The Trouble with Alice." *Reporter,* XXXII (January 28, 1965), 53–54.

Roth, Philip. "The Play That Dare Not Speak Its Name." *New York Review of Books,* IV, 2 (February 25, 1965), 4. Review of the book.

Sheed, Wilfred. "The Stage." *Commonweal,* LXXXI (January 22, 1965), 543.

Simon, John. "Theatre Chronicle." *Hudson Review,* XVIII (Spring 1965), 81–84.

Taubman, Howard. "Theatre: Albee's 'Tiny Alice' Opens." *New York Times* (December 30, 1964), 14.

——."Enigma That Runs Down." *New York Times* (January 10, 1965), section II, 1.

Secondary Sources

"Tinny Allegory." *Time,* LXXXV (January 8, 1965), 32.

Ulanov, Barry. "Luv *and* Tiny Alice." *Catholic World,* CC (March 1965), 383–84.

Watts, Richard Jr. "Edward Albee's Home of Secrets." *New York Post* (December 30, 1964). See *New York Theatre Critics' Reviews,* XXV (1964), 97.

Weintraub, S. *Books Abroad.* XXXIX (Autumn 1965), 459. Review of book.

World Theatre, XIV (May-June 1965), 317.

Zolotow, Sam. "Box-Office Queue for 'Tiny Alice.' " *New York Times* (December 31, 1964), 14.

Malcolm

Brustein, Robert. "Albee's Allegory of Innocence." *New Republic,* CLIV (January 29, 1966), 34, 36.

Choice: Books for College Libraries, III (September 1966), 534. Review of book.

Corrigan, Robert W. "Theatre: *Malcolm* 'didn't mean very much.' " *Vogue,* CXLVII (February 15, 1966), 56.

Deuel, Pauline. Short review of book *Malcolm* in *Books Abroad* (Winter 1967), 90.

Kauffman, Stanley. "Theater: Edward Albee's 'Malcolm.' " *New York Times* (January 12, 1966), 29.

"Malcolm Adapted by Edward Albee from the novel by James Purdy." Anonymous review of publication of play. *Virginia Quarterly Review,* XLIII (Winter 1967), xxi.

McCarten, John. "Innocent Astray." *New Yorker,* XLI (January 22, 1966), 74.

"The Murk of Albee." *Newsweek,* LXVIII (January 24, 1966), 82.

New York Theatre Critics'Reviews, XXVII, 1 (January 17 1966), 392–95.

Sheed, Wilfred. "Notes on Albee." *Commonweal,* LXXXIII (February 18, 1966), 584–85.

"Tiny Albee." *Time,* LXXXVII (January 21, 1966), 50.

World Premières, XV, 2 (1966), 181–82.

Wortis, Irving. *Library Journal,* XCI (June 1, 1966), 2868. Review of book.

A Delicate Balance

Brustein, Robert. "Albee Decorates an Old House." *New Republic,* CLV (October 8, 1966), 35–36.

Clurman, Harold. "Theatre." *Nation,* CCIII (October 10, 1966), 361–63.

——."Albee on Balance." *New York Times,* Sunday drama section (November 13, 1966), 1, 3.

Cooke, Richard P. "The Theater: Albee's Latest." *Wall Street Journal* (September 26, 1966).

Croce, Arlene. "New-Old, Old-New, and New." *National Review,* XIX (January 24, 1967), 99–100.

"Dialogue Takes Charge in New Albee Play." *London Times* (October 10, 1966), 6.

Hardwick, Elizabeth. "Straight Play: A Delicate Balance." *New York Review of Books,* VII (October 20, 1966), 4–5. Review of book.

Hewes, Henry. "The Family That Stayed Separate." *Saturday Review,* XLIX (October 8, 1966), 90.

Kemper, Robert Graham. "A Weekend with the 'Can do' Family." *Christian Century,* LXXXIII (November 23, 1966), 1447.

Kerr, Walter. "The Theater: Albee's 'A Delicate Balance.' "

Secondary Sources

New York Times (September 23, 1966), 44L. See
Sunday drama section (October 9, 1966), 10–11,
for reaction to this review.

Kitching, J. *Publishers' Weekly,* CXC (October 10, 1966),
72. Review of book.

Lewis, Theophilus. "A Delicate Balance." *America,* CXV
(October 8, 1966), 432–33.

McCarten, John. "Six on a Seesaw." *New Yorker,* XLII
(October 1, 1966), 121.

Nadel, Norman."'A Delicate Balance' Lacks it." *New
York World Journal Tribune* (September 23, 1966),
See *New York Theatre Critics' Reviews,* XXVII
(1966), 295.

National Review, XIX (January 24, 1967), 99.

Nelson, Gerald. "Edward Albee and His Well-Made Plays."
Tri-Quarterly, 5 (1966), 182–88.

New York Theatre Critics'Reviews, XXVII (1966),
294–297. Newspaper reviews by Walter Kerr, Richard
Watts Jr., John Chapman, Richard P. Cooke, and
Martin Gottfried.

Pryce-Jones, Alan. "The Theatre of Edward Albee."
Listener, LXXVI (November 24, 1966), 763–64.

Prideaux, Tom. "A Cry of Loss: 'Dilemma Come Back!' "
Life, LXI (October 28, 1966), 119.

Rachow, L.A. *Library Journal,* XCII (February 1, 1967),
594. Review of book.

Roddy, Joseph. "The Night of the Brawl." *Look,* XXX, 3
(1966), 42–48.

Roud, Richard. "A Successful Failure." *Manchester
Guardian* (October 13, 1966), 9.

Sheed, Wilfred. "Liquor Is Thicker." *Commonweal,*
LXXXV (October 14, 1966), 55–56.

Simon, John. "Theatre Chronicle." *Hudson Review,* XIX
    (Winter 1966-67), 627–29.

"Skin Deep." *Newsweek,* LXVIII (October 3, 1966), 98.

Weales, Gerald. "Stop the Balance, I Want to Get Off."
    Reporter, XXXV (October 20, 1966), 52–53.

Weintraub, Stanley. Short review of book *A Delicate
    Balance. Books Abroad* (Summer 1967), 346.

West, Anthony. "Theatre: *A Delicate Balance,* 'Self-
    Indulgent.' " *Vogue,* CXLVIII (November 1, 1966),
    150.

"Whiskey Before Breakfast." *Time,* LXXXVIII (September
    30, 1966), 88.

Everything in the Garden

Brustein, Robert. "Albee at the Crossroads." *New Republic,*
    CLVII (December 16, 1967), 25–27.

Clurman, Harold. "Theatre." *Nation,* CCV (December 18,
    1967), 669.

Hewes, Henry. "A Hothouse Is Not a Home." *Saturday
    Review,* L. (December 16, 1967), 24.

Kroll, Jack. "Poisoned Quills." *Newsweek,* LXX
    (December 11, 1967), 96.

La Fontane, Barbara. "Triple Threat on, Off and Off-Off
    Broadway." *New York Times* (February 25, 1968),
    36–37, 39, 40, 42, 44, 46.

Lewis, Theophilus. "Everything in the Garden." *America,*
    CXVIII (January 6, 1968), 19–20.

New York Theatre Critics' Reviews, XXVIII (1967),
    204–05, 211–13. Reviews by Walter Kerr, Clive
    Barnes, Richard Watts Jr., Martin Gottfried, Richard
    P. Cooke, Douglas Watt.

Secondary Sources

"On Broadway: Tattletale-Grey Comedy." *Time,* XC (December 8, 1967), 96.

Prideaux, Tom. "Why Must I Worry About Albee?" *Life* (February 2, 1968), 16.

Simon, John. "Albee's Necrosis." *Commonweal,* LXXXVII (January 12, 1968), 444, 446.

Weales, Gerald. "Working Wives." *Reporter,* XXXVII (December 28, 1967), 38–39.

West, Anthony. "Albee's Innocence," *Vogue,* CLI (January 15, 1968), 28.

Box and Quotations from Chairman Mao Tse-tung

Barnes, Clive. "Theatre: Albee's Adventurous Plays." *New York Times* (October 1, 1968), 39.

Clurman, Harold. "Theatre." *Nation,* CCVI (March 25, 1968), 420.

Hewes, Henry. "Woman Overboard." *Saturday Review,* LI (March 23, 1968), 34.

Kroll, Jack. "Inside the Cube." *Newsweek,* LXXI (March 28, 1968), 109.

Germany, Austria, and Switzerland

Primary Sources

(Arranged chronologically)

PLAYS

"Die Zoogeschichte." *Theatrum Mundi: amerikanische Dramen der Gegenwart.* Frankfurt am Main: S. Fischer Verlag, 1961, 427–450. Anthology.

"Der amerikanische Traum." *Theater im S. Fischer Verlag I.* Frankfurt am Main: S. Fischer Verlag, 1962, 399–433. Anthology.

Der amerikanische Traum. Der Tod von Bessie Smith. Die Zoogeschichte. Der Sandkasten. Frankfurt am Main: S. Fischer Verlag, 1962.

Wer hat Angst vor Virginia Woolf? Frankfurt am Main: S. Fischer Verlag, 1963.

Die Ballade vom traurigen Café. Frankfurt am Main: S. Fischer Verlag, 1964.

"Wer hat Angst vor Virginia Woolf?" *Spectaculum 7.* Stuttgart: Suhrkamp Verlag, 1964, 7–101. Anthology of modern plays.

Winzige Alice. Frankfurt am Main: S. Fischer Verlag, 1965. Actors' edition.

"Winzige Alice." *Theater 1966 Chronik und Bilanz eines Buehnenjahres,* special yearly issue of *Theater heute,* August 20, 1966, 85–103.

Empfindliches Gleichgewicht. Winzige Alice. Frankfurt am Main: S. Fischer Verlag, 1967.

Proposed editions:

Friedrichs Dramatiker des Welttheaters: Albee. Velber: Friedrich Verlag, Fall 1968. Collected works.

Edward Albee At Home And Abroad

Albees gesammelte Dramen. Frankfurt am Main: S. Fischer Verlag, Fall 1968.

Secondary Sources
(Arranged alphabetically)

GENERAL

"Aus New York." *Theater heute,* IX, iii (1968), 39.

Braun, Pinkas. "Etwas ueber Edward Albee," *Burgtheater im Akademietheater* (Wien), Programmheft (1967).

"Edward Albee in der Sowjetunion." *Frankfurter Rundschau,* February 5, 1963.

jw. "Apartes Spiel im Souterrain," *Bayerische Staats-Zeitung* (Muenchen), June 10, 1966.

"Notizen." *Theater heute,* IX, v (1968), 34.

Paetel, Karl O. "Albee und das Absurde," *Die Furche* (Wien), No. 40 (1965).

Ratner, Mark C. "Edward Albee," *Stadttheater Ingolstadt,* Programmheft (1966/1967).

Schulz-Seitz, Ruth Eva. *Edward Albee—der Dichterphilosoph der Buehne.* Frankfurt am Main: Vittorio Klostermann, 1966.

"Shakespeare liegt immer vorn—was wird am meisten gespielt?" *Theater heute,* VIII, i (1967), 47.

Skow, John. "Amerikas aggressivster Broadway-Star: Edward Albee—ein Poet des Hasses," *Die Weltwoche* (Zuerich), January 31, 1964. American critic.

Wanderscheck, Hermann. "Das Theater in New York," *Der Literat* (Frankfurt am Main), No. 7 (1965).

The Zoo Story

B., Dr. "Argumente fuer den Freitod," *Hamburger Echo,* December 11, 1959.

Bayer, E. Hennemann. "Studio fuer Stuttgarter
Staatsbuehne: Zum Naechsten hin fuehrt kein Weg,"
Abendpost (Frankfurt am Main), February 20, 1960.

b-ch. " 'The Zoo-story' in Heilbronn," *Stuttgarter Zeitung,*
April 7, 1967.

be. "Triumph der Komoedie," *Stuttgarter Zeitung,*
December 15, 1959.

Besch, K. "Freiburger Kammertheater: Zwei Einakter
von Albee," *Badische Neueste Nachrichten*
(Karlsruhe), February 7, 1964.

bl. " 'Ein Stueck muss unter die Haut gehen': Stuttgarter
Tourneetheater fuehrt 'Die Zoogeschichte' von Albee
auf," *Cannstatter Zeitung,* May 1, 1963.

Burschel, Rudolf. " 'Denke mehr an deinen Naechsten,' "
Allgemeine Zeitung (Freiburg), January 11, 1964.

D. "Premieren in Baden-Baden," *Stuttgarter Zeitung,*
October 27, 1959.

Dannenberg, Peter. "Monologe allein und zu zweit,"
VZ-Kieler Morgenzeitung, October 29, 1965.

"Doch noch Auffuehrungen." *Allgemeine Zeitung*
(Freiburg), January 20, 1964.

Drews, Wolfgang. Critical review, *Frankfurter Allgemeine,*
April 27, 1960.

"Edward Albee: 'Die Zoo-Geschichte'." Excerpts from
reviews by Wolfgang Schimming, Willy H. Thiem
(see Thiem), Georg Zivier, Florian Kienzl and Roe,
Volksbuehnenspiegel, IV, i (1960), 16.

ek. "Bankkrach im Park," *Schwaebische Donau-Zeitung*
(Ulm), August 23, 1965.

epl. " 'Zoo-Geschichte' in Kaiserslautern: Zwischen Liebe
und Hass ist nur ein noch feiger Kompromiss,"
Abendpost (Frankfurt am Main), January 21, 1960.

Secondary Sources

Feri. "Feri schaut hinter die Kulissen," *Telegraf* (Berlin), October 15, 1961.

G.R. "Dramatische 'Endspiele' des Lebens," *Der Mittag* (Duesseldorf), February 26, 1962.

Giessler, Rupert, Dr. "Edward Albee —amerikanisch und deutsch," *Badische Zeitung* (Freiburg), January 11, 1964.

gr. "John Mortimer und Edward Albee," *Wuerttembergische Staatstheater Stuttgart Kammertheater*, Programmheft enclosure (1960).

H. "Konstruierte 'Zoogeschichte,' " *Westfaelische Zeitung* (Guetersloh), March 27, 1963.

H.J. "Vorstellung in deutsch und englisch," *Heidelberger Tageblatt*, February 24, 1964.

H.S. "Bankgespraeche," *Neue Ruhr-Zeitung* (Essen), March 9, 1962.

HA. "Einakter im 'theater 53'," *Hamburger Abendblatt*, December 13, 1959.

hb. "Zoogeschichte im Amerika-Haus," *Sueddeutsche Zeitung* (Muenchen), April 4, 1964.

Hensel, Georg. "Nach den Physikern die Affen. Darmstaedter Premiere: Duerrenmatt, Albees 'Zoogeschichte' und Kafka," *Die Welt*, February 3, 1967.

——:"Theatralisches Vivarium: 'Die Zoogeschichte' von Edward Albee und 'Ein Bericht fuer eine Akademie' von Franz Kafka im Darmstaedter Theater im Schloss," *Darmstaedter Echo*, January 23, 1967.

Hurck, Walter. "Alter Shaw, junger Albee," *Ruhr-Nachrichten Essener Tageblatt*, March 8, 1962.

Iden, Peter, "Gesellschaft—auf den Affen gekommen," *Frankfurter Rundschau*, January 31, 1967.

53

j. b. Review *Oldenburgisches Staatstheater,* Programmheft
15 (1961).

J. K. "Ist Realismus eigentlich modern?" *Sueddeutsche
Zeitung* (Muenchen), April 4, 1960.

Katschinski, Claus. " 'Man muss die Folgen seiner
Handlungen erkennen': Zwei Einakter von Albee und
Kafka—ein Hoehepunkt der Spielzeit," *Cuxhavener
Presse,* February 15, 1966.

Kesting, Marianne. *Panorama des zeitgenoessischen
Theaters.* Muenchen: R. Piper & Co. Verlag, 1962,
196–198.

Kienzl, Florian. "Berliner Zwischenbilanz," *Stuttgarter
Zeitung,* October 7, 1959.

Kirsch, Siegfried. "Im kleinen Kreis egoistischer Interessen,"
Ruesselheimer Echo, March 9, 1964.

Klaus, Rudolf U. "Zur 'Zoo-Geschichte,' " *Atelier
Theater am Naschmarkt* (Wein), Programmheft 2
(1960).

Kollakowsky, Norbert. "Edward Albees Zoogeschichte,"
Studio '66 (Verden), Studioheft 2 (1965/1966).

kr. "Unruhe im Gehege der Selbstzufriedenheit:
Spielzeiteroeffnung mit Edward Albees 'Zoogeschi-
chte' in Ulm," *Schwaebische Zeitung* (Leutkirch),
August 24, 1965.

Lengsfeld, Jochen. "Egoismus oder Unverstand,"
Saarbruecker Landeszeitung, November 29, 1966.

Lewinsky, Charles. "Zu diesem Abend," *Werkstattbuehne*
(Ingolstadt), Programmheft W3 (1967/1968).

Liedtke, Hans Juergen. "Zu Edward Albees 'Die
Zoogeschichte,' " *Landestheater Darmstadt 1966/
1967 Theater im Schloss,* Programmheft.

Lietzmann, Sabina. "Zwischen Central Park und Dschungel.

Berliner Festwochen-Erfolge," *Frankfurter Allgemeine,* October 6, 1959.

Ludewig, Horst. "Edward Albee oder das billige Argument," *Nordwestdeutsche Rundschau* (Wilhelmshaven), March 4, 1963.

Luyken, Sonja. "Neues Stueck von Tankred Dorst in Bielefeld: Ein Gefangener pro Waerter ist kein unbilliges Verlangen," *Abendpost* (Frankfurt am Main), November 22, 1960.

Menck, Clara. "Vorboten neuer Romantik," *Frankfurter Allgemeine,* February 19, 1960.

Meyer, A., Dr. "Verzweifelte Einsamkeit," *Main-Post* (Wuerzburg), September 28, 1963.

Moerschbach, Fritz. "Jedes Laecheln wird zur Fratze," *Neue Rhein-Zeitung* (Koeln), October 5, 1962.

Nolte, Jost. "Ueberdrehter Dreh," *Die Welt* (Hamburg), December 11, 1959.

"Notizen." *Theater heute,* IV, vi (1963), 54–55.

Pesch, Hans Karl. "Traum oder Trauma?" *Rheinische Post* (Duesseldorf), November 16, 1962).

Peters, Wolfgang A. "Jerry und ein Mann namens Krapp," *Frankfurter Allgemeine,* October 30, 1959.

Peuckert, Hannes. "Studio-Eroeffnung mit Urauffuehrung: Erfolgreiches Experiment mit Einaktern von Dorst und Albee," *Westfalen-Blatt* (Bielefeld), November 21, 1960.

Prem, Friedrich. "Freiheit und Notwendigkeit—Anpassung und Widerstand," *Das Schauspiel Cuxhaven,* Programmheft 5 (1965/1966).

r. "Zimmertheater-Premiere in Tuebingen: 'Die Zoo-Geschichte' und 'Der Sarghaendler,' " *Schwaebische Zeitung* (Leutkirch), March 14, 1961.

Rehn, Jens. "Zweimal schwarzes Licht," *Schillertheater* (Berlin), Programmheft 87 (1959/1960); *Studio* (Kiel), Programmheft (1962/1963).

Richter, Wolfgang. "Aachener Kammerspiele: Geschichte vom einsamen Menschen," *Eifeler Volkszeitung* (Schleiden), July 1, 1963.

Sahl, Hans. "Flucht vor der Existenz," *Die Welt* (Berlin), June 29, 1963.

Sawatzki, Guenter. "Kann man dichten lernen?" *Theater heute*, III, viii (1962), 20–22.

Schirmer, Editha. "Die 'Zoogeschichte' endet schockierend," *Nordwestdeutsche Rundschau* (Wilhelmshaven), March 29, 1961.

Schn., D. "Albees 'Zoogeschichte,' " *Stuttgarter Nachrichten,* March 14, 1967.

Stephan, Heinz. "Zweimal Edward Albee," *Koelnische Rundschau,* October 5, 1962.

tg. " 'Mensch, hoer dir das an!' " *Schwaebisches Tagblatt* (Tuebingen), March 11, 1961.

Thiem, Willy H. "Barlogs Werkraumtheater: Aussenseiter zogen Bilanz," *Abendpost* (Frankfurt am Main), October 1, 1959.

U. G., Dr. "Kulturbrief aus Bielefeld," *Die Glocke* (Oelde), November 23, 1960.

W.F. "Kontaktlos bis zum Untergang," *Die Welt* (Essen), October 20, 1962.

Westecker, Wilhelm. "Studiobuehne in Stuttgart," *Der Tagesspiegel* (Berlin), April 29, 1960.

Williams, Laura. "Dem sogenannten Nichts gegenueber," *Ulmer Theater,* Programmheft 15 (1965). Translated from the American by Renate Voss.

The Sand Box

Althoff, Juergen. "Neue Stuecke in Bremerhaven: Das Warten im Sandkasten," *Abendpost* (Frankfurt am Main), May 28, 1963.

Berndt, Hans. "Bittere Rosinen: Amerikanische Einakter in Bremerhaven," *Weser-Kurier* (Bremen), December 22, 1962.

——:"Kritischer Rundblick ueber Schauspiel: Bremerhaven," *Theater heute*, IV, ii (1963), 48.

"Grausamkeit und Anteilnahme." *Schauspielgruppe Dr. Elrod* (Kreuzlingen), Programmheft (1965).

Hentschel, Peter. "Kalter, toedlicher Witz: Albees 'Sandkasten' erstaufgefuehrt," *Die Welt* (Berlin), December 31, 1962.

Horn, Effi. "Buechner-Theater: Partiegefuehle beim Sandkasten," *Muenchner Merkur*, May 23, 1966.

Linder, Hans. "Im Kleinen Haus: Vier amerikanische Versuche," *Bremerhavener Buergerzeltung*, December 29, 1962.

Rhode, Werner. "Oma im Sandkasten: Einakter aus Amerika in Bremerhaven," *Deutsche Zeitung mit Wirtschaftszeitung* (Koeln), December 27, 1962.

The Death of Bessie Smith

Becher, Carl J. "Szenische Experimente?" *Frankfurter Rundschau*, March 11, 1967.

Braun, Hanns. "Die Schaubuehne als Pranger," *Sueddeutsche Zeitung* (Muenchen), March 6, 1964.

Detlefsen, Jorgen. "Bessie Smith lebt!" *Suedschleswigsche Heimatzeitung* (Flensburg), November 27, 1964.

"Edward Albee: Der Tod von Bessie Smith." Exerpts from

reviews by G. Wandel, R.M., Manfred Moschner,
Kurt Habernoll, Werner Fiedler, and Felix Henseleit,
Volksbuehnenspiegel, VI, vii/viii (1960), 18.

Fischer, Thea. "Heikle Dramatik aus England und USA:
Triumph der Menschenwuerde im Schauspielhaus
Bochum mit Lessings 'Nathan,' " *Westfaelische
Rundschau* (Dortmund), November 1, 1960.

Ga., Dr. " 'Der Tod der Bessie Smith,' " *Flensburger
Tageblatt,* November 27, 1964.

Georgi, Malte. "Hamburger Theaterbrief: Auftakt mit
Moliere und Shakespeare," *Heidenheimer Zeitung,*
September 19, 1962

hd. "Einmal ernst—einmal heiter," *Fraenkische Landeszeitung Dinkelsbuehl,* October 7, 1966.

Henning, Erhard. "Hamburger Theaterbrief: Grosse Ehre
fuer kleines Theater," *Frankfurter Neue Presse,*
January 3, 1963.

Hofman, Will. "Hamburger Kulturspiegel," *Norddeutsche
Nachrichten* (Hamburg), September 7, 1962.

Horn, Effi. "Theater an der Leopoldstrasse: Tankred
Dorst und Edward Albee. Schmaehende Ingrid—
hysterische Lachtaube," *Muenchner Merkur,* March 6,
1964.

H–t. "Probleme auf kleiner Flamme," *Kieler Nachrichten,*
December 17, 1962.

"In Berlin holte Barlog auf." *Die Buehne,* Heft 21 (1960),
26.

Jacobs, Wilhelm. "Thalia-Theater und das Theater im
Zimmer eroeffneten die Saison: Zwei Hamburger
Schauspielpremieren," *Braunschweiger Zeitung,*
September 11, 1962.

Jenke, Manfred. "Kritik und Information: Hamburg,"

Secondary Sources

Theater heute, III, x (1962), 38.

Karsch, Walter. "Dramatik von vorgestern," *Der Tagesspiegel* (Berlin), April 23, 1960.

Kienzl, Florian. "Grauen zweier Zeiten," *Stuttgarter Zeitung,* May 17, 1960.

Klaus, Rudolf U. "Zum 'Tod von Bessie Smith,' " *Ateliertheater* (Wein), Programmheft 2 (1960).

L. O. "Respekt vor der kleinen Form: Einakter von Hermann Moers und Edward Albee im Theater am Goetheplatz," *Hessische Allgemeine* (Kassel), March 26, 1963.

Luft, Friedrich. "Die neue Dreigroschenoper von Ostberlin," *Sueddeutsche Zeitung* (Muenchen), April 28, 1960.

"Nach dem Schock eine befreiende Posse." *Hohenloher Tagblatt* (Crailsheim), October 7, 1966.

Nebelung, Joerg Peter. "Zu unserer Studioreihe moderner Dramatik," *Nordmark-Landestheater Schleswig,* Programmheft 3 (1965/1966).

Ny. "Import aus England und USA: Einakter von Pinter und Albee in den Kammerspielen," *Ruhr-Nachrichten* (Dortmund), October 28, 1960.

P.D. "Lehrstueck und Leerstueck," *VZ Kieler Morgenzeitung,* December 17, 1962.

Rade, Heinz. "Koenig Behringer und Kaiserin Bessie Smith," *Stuttgarter Nachrichten,* March 12, 1964.

Ruhrberg, Karl. "Zwei Einakter—ein Treffer: Stuecke von Harold Pinter und Edward Albee in Bochum," *Duesseldorfer Nachrichten,* October 29, 1960.

Schuch, Wolfgang. "Ein Albee fuer uns: 'Der Tod von Bessie Smith' in Greifswald," *Theater der Zeit,* XXII, xiv (1967).

Tank, Kurt Lothar. "Hamburger Theaterbeginn Sieg der 300jaehrigen," *Sonntagsblatt* (Hamburg), September 16, 1962.

Trippler, Hans Joachim. "Mordbefehl kam aus dem Lift: Angelsaechsische Einakter in den Bochumer Kammerspielen," *Wanne-Eickeler Zeitung,* October 28, 1960.

Tynan, Kenneth. "New York: Kenneth Tynan berichtet ueber die Spielzeit 1960/1961," *Theater heute,* II, v (1961), 40–41. English critic.

uenn. "Kieler Theaterbrief: Junge Autoren auf der Studio-buehne," *Schleswig-Holsteinische Landeszeitung* (Rendsburg), December 24, 1962.

Wanderscheck, Hermann. "Arthur Miller und Edward Albee greifen ins Heute," *Abendpost* (Frankfurt am Main), May 7, 1960.

——. "Miller —Albee —Williams," *Hamburger Abendblatt,* May 6, 1960.

The American Dream

"Ein amerikanischer Alptraum." *National-Zeitung* (Basel), June 6, 1963.

ASV. "Ein Goetzenbild," *Frankfurter Allgemeine,* January 9, 1962.

Berger, Friedrich. "Aber Oma braucht, bitte, ein richtiges Plueschsofa," *Koelner Stadtanzeiger,* October 5, 1962.

"Berliner Festwochen: Omas Traum." *Der Spiegel,* No. 43 (1961), 81–82.

Besch, K. "Freiburger Kammertheater: Zwei Einakter von Albee," *Badische Neueste Nachrichten* (Karlsruhe), February 7, 1964.

Billetter, Walter. "Der amerikanische Dramatiker Edward
Albee," *Komoedien-Werkstatt* (Basel), Programmheft
5 (1962/1963).

Bruees, Otto. "Ein Albtraum, sehr bunt, kaum aber ein
Regenbogen," *Der Mittag* (Duesseldorf), January 5,
1962.

Burschel, Rudolf. " 'Denke mehr an deinen Naechsten,' "
Allgemeine Zeitung (Freiburg), January 11, 1964.

"Drehbuehne." *Der Abend* (Berlin), October 17, 1961.

eb. "Die Traumwandler der Wohlstandsgesellschaft,"
Volksblatt (Bamberg), October 18, 1966.

Elsner, Hans. "Albee-Premiere in Basel: Oma rettet alles,"
Abendpost (Frankfurt am Main), June 15, 1963.

Giessler, Rupert, Dr. "Edward Albee—amerikanisch und
deutsch," *Badische Zeitung* (Freiburg), January 11,
1964.

H.J. "Vorstellung in deutsch und englisch," *Heidelberger
Tageblatt,* February 24, 1964.

Henning, Erhard. "Hamburger Theaterbrief: Grosse Ehre
fuer kleines Theater," *Frankfurter Neue Presse,*
January 3, 1963.

Hildebrandt, Traute. "Berliner Festwochen: Der Traum
vom starken Mann," *Muenchner Merkur,* October 10,
1961.

Hofman, Will. "Hamburger Kulturspiegel," *Norddeutsche
Nachrichten* (Hamburg), September 7, 1962.

Jacobs, Wilhelm. "Thalia-Theater und das Theater im
Zimmer eroeffneten die Saison: Zwei Hamburger
Schauspielpremieren," *Braunschweiger Zeitung,*
September 11, 1962.

Jenke, Manfred. "Kritik und Information: Hamburg,"
Theater heute, III, x (1962), 38.

Karsch, Walther. "Komoediantisches Feuerwerk in der Werkstatt," *Der Tagesspiegel* (Berlin), October 9, 1961.

Kaul, Walter. "Amerikanischer Alptraum," *Der Kurier* (Berlin), October 9, 1961.

Kesting, Marianne. *Panorama des zeitgenoessischen Theaters.* Muenchen: R. Piper & Co. Verlag, 1962, 196–198.

Klaus, Rudolf U. "Albee—oder: Traum und Albtraum Amerikas," *Komoedie Basel,* Programmheft 3 (1964/1965); *Bamberger Theater Blaetter,* Programmheft 2 (1966/1967).

Koch, Marianne. "Vom Theater zum Sechstagerennen: Ein gelungener Abend. . .," *B.Z.* (Berlin), October 9, 1961.

Kotschenreuther, Helmut. "Familienquintett unter Bosheit und Banalitaeten," *Neue Ruhr-Zeitung* (Essen), October 11, 1961.

——·"Premiere: Absurdes Theater, Barlog inszenierte Albee 'Amerikanischen Traum' —Ausklang der Berliner Festwochen," *Frankfurter Nachtausgabe,* October 11, 1961.

Ludewig, Horst. "Edward Albee oder das billige Argument," *Nordwestdeutsche Rundschau* (Wilhelmshaven), March 4, 1963.

Luft, Friedrich. "Satirische Selbstbezichtigung," *Mykenae Theater-Korrespondenz,* No. 8 (1961); *Tribuene* (Duesseldorf), Programmheft 2 (1961/1962).

Mannstaedt, Max Heinz. "Edward Albee blieb auf der Strecke," *(Grafschafter Nachrichten* (Nordhorn), December 5, 1962.

Moerschbach, Fritz. "Jedes Laecheln wird zur Fratze,"

Secondary Sources

Neue Rhein-Zeitung (Koeln), October 5, 1962.

Niehoff, Karena. "Deutsche Autoren—Fehlanzeige,"
Stuttgarter Nachrichten, October 17, 1961.

Pesch, Hans Karl. "Traum oder Trauma?" *Rheinische Post*
(Duesseldorf), November 16, 1962.

Pfeiffer, Herbert. "Die neue amerikanische Gesellschaft,"
Berliner Morgenpost, October 10, 1961.

Rech, Kurt. "Dichter und Taenzer," *Berliner Morgenpost,*
October 7, 1961.

Ruhrberg, Karl. "Lebensleere—satirisch entlarvt,"
Duesseldorfer Nachrichten, January 5, 1962.

Sahl, Hans. "Probleme im Breitwandformat," *Die Welt*
(Berlin), March 27, 1961.

Sch., Dr. "Zorniger Autor klagt die Gesellschaft an,"
Fraenkischer Tag (Bamberg), October 17, 1966.

Schimming, Wolfgang. "Liebe Familie," *Der Abend*
(Berlin), October 9, 1961.

Schmidt, Otto. " 'Der Amerikanische Traum,' "
Bamberger Volksblatt, October 13, 1966.

Schuller, Renate. "Von Spielern, Spinnern und
Spitzenhaeubchen," *Saarbruecker Zeitung,* May 22,
1964.

Stange, C.R. " 'Der amerikanische Traum,' " *Basler
Nachrichten,* June 6, 1963.

Stephan, Heinz. "Zweimal Edward Albee," *Koelnische
Rundschau,* October 5, 1962.

Tank, Kurt Lothar. "Hamburger Theaterbeginn Sieg der
300jaehrigen," *Sonntagsblatt* (Hamburg), September
16, 1962.

ten. "Absurdes Theater in Berlin," *Frankfurter Rundschau,*
October 13, 1961.

Thiem, Willy H. "Das Stueck weist ins Allgemeine,"

63

Die Mykenae Theater-Korrespondenz, No. 8 (1961)‏; *Tribuene* (Duesseldorf), Programmheft 2 (1961/1962); *Bamberger Theater Blaetter,* Programmheft 2 (1966/1967), enclosure.

Tynan, Kenneth. "New York: Kenneth Tynan berichtet ueber die Spielzeit 1960/1961," *Theater heute,* II, v (1961), 40–41. English critic.

Vielhaber, Gerd. "Nicht die Klaue des Loewen," *Koelner Stadtanzeiger,* January 6, 1962.

Wanderscheck, Hermann. "Kontaktlosigkeit der Menschen," *Die Mykenae Theater-Korrespondenz,* No. 8 (1961); *Tribuene* (Duesseldorf), Programmheft 2 (1961/1962).

W-g. "Hohlkoepfe am heiteren Spiegel: 'Der amerikanische Traum' von Albee in der 'Werkstatt,' " *Spandauer Volksblatt* (Berlin), October 10, 1961.

Who's Afraid of Virginia Woolf?

a. " 'Wer hat Angst vor Virginia Woolf?' " *Duesseldorfer Wochenspiegel,* 8 (1965), 15, 18.

-a. "Amerikanisches Laientheater zeigt Mut: Halbtagsmimen mit grosser Literatur," *Der Kurier* (Berlin), November 11, 1963.

"Albee: Folter am Herd." *Der Spiegel,* No. 43 (1963), 110–112.

"Angst vor amerikanischen Lebensformen?" *Pforzheimer Zeitung,* April 18, 1964.

ASV. "Ruede Groesse." *Frankfurter Allgemeine,* April 8, 1965.

Azi. "Grandioser Erfolg des Hamburger Schauspielhauses: Nur sich zu hassen, sind sie da," *Luebecker Morgen,* April 14, 1964.

Secondary Sources

B., Dr. "Albees Alptraum," *Kieler Nachrichten,* November
11, 1966.

Bassler, Hansgeorg. "Ein wahres Inferno an Seelengemetzel,"
Pfaelzische Volkszeitung (Kaiserslautern), March 20,
1965.

be. "Keine Angst vor Virginia Woolf," *Stuttgarter Zeitung,*
June 23, 1966.

Beckmann, Heinz. "Hoellenfahrt durch eine Ehe," *Madame,*
No. 11, (1963).

——:"Provokation und Evokation," *Theater heute,* VII,
xii (1966), 5–7.

Berg, Robert von. "Weder absurd noch realistisch,"
Sueddeutsche Zeitung (Muenchen), February 12,
1963.

——:"Wer hat Angst vor Edward Albee," reprinted in
"Aufgelesen," *Theater heute,* IV, vi (1963), 3.

Bischof, A. "Eis-Traenen unterm·Whisky," *Aachener
Nachrichten,* September 29, 1964.

Blaha, Paul. "Toedliche Gesellschaftsspiele," *Kurier*
(Wein), April 17, 1964.

Brockmann, Eva. "Hamburg: Ehe in den Fesseln der
Zivilisation," *Die Andere Zeitung* (Hamburg),
April 23, 1964.

bs. "Neu im Stadttheater: 'Wer hat Angst vor Virginia
Woolf?' Am Montagabend Premiere," *Donau-Kurier*
(Ingolstadt), October 1, 1966.

Burschel, Rudolf. "Dem Publikum wird nichts geschenkt,"
*Suedwestdeutsche Allgemeine Zeitung und Rundschau
fuer Freiburg und Suedbaden* (Freiburg), October 7,
1966.

Canaris, Volker. "Kritische Chronik: Bonn," *Theater
heute,* VIII, i (1967), 55–56.

Colberg, Klaus. "Stadttheater Ingolstadt: Gesellschafts-
spiel in der Hoelle," *Donau-Kurier* (Ingolstadt),
October 5, 1966.

Cordes, I. "Edward Albee grossartig interpretiert,"
Niederelbe Zeitung (Otterndorf), November 29, 1966.

D. W. "Die Nacht der Selbstzerfleischung," *Westdeutsche
Zeitung* (Krefeld), April 10, 1967.

——:"Zum 50. Male 'Wer hat Angst vor Virginia Woolf . .' "
Die Welt (Berlin), April 13, 1964.

Dannenberg, Peter. "Buehnen der Landeshauptstadt Kiel:
Ein amerikanischer Albtraum," *VZ Kieler
Morgenzeitung,* October 19, 1964.

"Diese Taylor wird die Welt schockieren." *Quick,* No. 26
(1966), 16–19.

DS. "Versoehnung aus Verzweiflung," *Frankfurter
Rundschau,* December 4, 1965.

e. a. j. "Grosser Erfolg: 'Virginia Woolf,' " *Suedwestdeutsche Allgemeine Zeitung Tageszeitung fuer
Mannheim und Nordbaden* (Mannheim), September
21, 1966.

E. H. "Bilder der US-Gesellschaft," *Die Andere Zeitung*
(Hamburg), June 9, 1966.

e. w. "Tendenzen im Drama— ein Ueberblick," *Theater
1963 Chronik und Bilanz eines Buehnenjahres,*
special yearly issue of *Theater heute,* August 20,
1963, 75–78.

Emigholz, Erich. "Albees 'Virginia Woolf' in den Kammerspielen: Angst um die Menschheit," *Bremer
Nachrichten,* November 8, 1965.

F. H. "Ehe-Hoelle wie noch nie!" *Hamburger Morgenpost,*
April 14, 1964.

Faber, Karin von. "Schock gegen Krise," *Kristall,*

No. 9 (1966), 26.

Ferber, Christian. "Seelensaltos aus dem Stand," *Die Welt* (Hamburg), April 14, 1964.

Fischer, I., Dr. "Im Suff hingeschwaetzte Tragoedie," *Heilbronner Stimme,* March 16, 1966.

G. " 'Wer hat Angst vor Virginia Woolf?' " *Badische Neueste Nachrichten* (Karlsruhe), June 30, 1964.

Gehl, Imke. "Tot wider Willen," *Bremer Nachrichten,* April 9, 1965.

——" 'Wer hat Angst vor Virginia Woolf . . .?' in Hamburg: Albees Walpurgisnacht," *Bremer Nachrichten,* April 14, 1964.

George, Manfred. "Vitriol in die Seelen," *Saarbruecker Zeitung,* December 22, 1962.

Giessler, Rupert, Dr. "Ein Spiel auf Leben und Tod," *Badische Zeitung* (Freiburg), October 7, 1966.

Gilles, Werner. "Eine amerikanische Walpurgisnacht," *Mannheimer Morgen,* May 31, 1966.

"Glossarium." *Theater heute,* IX, vi (1968), 41.

Gneuss, Christian. "Skandinavische Notizen," *Theater heute,* VI, vii (1965), 30–32.

Golitschek, Joseph von. "Das Ende aller Illusionen," *Heidelberger Tageblatt,* October 22, 1964.

Graeser, Leonhardt. "Kammerspiele Muenchen: Wer hat Angst vor Virginia Woolf?—Mit Messer und Sonde," *8-Uhr-Blatt* (Nuernberg), October 24, 1963.

Grimme, Karl Maria. "Sex, vivisektorisch gesehen," *Neue Blaetter des Theaters in der Josefstadt* (Wein), Programmheft 12 (1963/1964).

H. "Schwarze Orchidee mit rosa Schimmer," *Die Rheinpfalz* (Ludwigshafen), May 31, 1966.

H.K. "Amerikanische Gesellschaftsspiele: Albees neue

'Buechse der Pandora' in Oberhausens Kulturwoche,"
Ruhrwacht (Oberhausen), December 9, 1963.

H. W. K. "Frohes Fest mit 'Virginia Woolf'!" *Generalanzeiger der Stadt Wuppertal,* December 22, 1965.

Hambach, Wilhelm, Dr. "Eine dreistuendige Eheschlacht,"
Flensburger Tageblatt, December 1, 1964.

Hampel, Norbert, Dr. "Ein Super-Strindberg aus Amerika,"
Nordwest-Zeitung (Oldenburg), March 18, 1967.

Harms, Claus. ". . . und doch glueht ein Funke Hoffnung,"
Hannoversche Allgemeine Zeitung, March 1, 1966.

" 'Heiter und grausam' soll es sein," *Dill-Zeitung*
(Dillenburg), February 8, 1963.

Hellwag, Sabine. " 'Kratz' die Etiketté ab,' " *Hannoversche
Presse,* March 1, 1966.

Hepp, Fred, Dr. "Muenchner Theaterzettel: Keine Angst
vor Virginia Woolf," *Augsburger Allgemeine,*
November 4, 1963.

Herchenroede, Jan. " 'Wer hat Angst vor Virginia Woolf?' "
Luebecker Nachrichten, November 11, 1966.

Herrmann, Walter M. "Zum erstenmal am Besenbinderhof:
Totentanz mit anderen Mitteln," *Hamburger
Abendblatt,* April 13, 1964.

Herrmann, Wilhelm. "Auf zum letzten Ehegefecht!"
Weser-Kurier (Bremen), November 8, 1965.

——:"Erfolg als Religion," *Weser-Kurier* (Bremen),
April 14, 1964.

Hildebrandt, Dieter. "Edward Albee und die Hexen,"
Stadttheater Bremerhaven 1964/65, Programmheft
15, enclosure.

Hn. "Muenchner Theaterbrief," *Trostberger Tagblatt,*
November 19, 1963.

Hoefler, Wolfgang. "Pathologische Studie im Vordergrund,"

Secondary Sources

Pirmasenser Zeitung, June 2, 1966.

Hofman, Will. "Hamburger Kulturspiegel: Es ist eine Orgie des Hasses," *Norddeutsche Nachrichten* (Hamburg), April 17, 1964.

H-t. "Edward Albee und das moderne Leben," *Kieler Nachrichten,* October 19, 1964.

hu. "Edward Albee auf Band," *Frankfurter Allgemeine,* March 12, 1964.

Huber, Werner. "Stadttheater Regensburg: 'Wer hat Angst vor Virginia Woolf?' von Albee," *Altmuehl-Bote* (Kehlheim), September 23, 1966.

Huebner, Paul. "Blaehung mit Whisky," *Rheinische Post* (Duesseldorf), April 5, 1965.

Hy. "Amerikanische Lebensprobleme—sehr aktuell," *Wiesbadener Tagblatt,* March 5, 1964.

Iden, Peter. "Schritte knirschen auf Glasscherben," *Frankfurter Rundschau,* October 23, 1963.

J. F. "Makabre Gesellschaftsspiele," *Badische Volkszeitung* (Karlsruhe), June 30, 1964.

Jacobs, Wilhelm. "Blick in eine Hoelle," *Frankfurter Rundschau,* April 17, 1964.

JvC. "Virginia Woolf in Mannheim," *Heidelberger Tageblatt,* June 24, 1966.

K. F. "Sich zueinander quaelen," *Schwaebische Donauzeitung* (Ulm), March 7, 1967.

K. K. "Angst vor Virginia Woolf?" *Suedwestdeutsche Allgemeine Zeitung Tageszeitung fuer Mannheim und Nordbaden* (Mannheim), June 29, 1966.

——."Nur Selbstzerfleischung?" *Frankfurter Allgemeine,* September 23, 1964.

Kaiser, Joachim. "Theater-Tagebuch," *Der Monat,* 186 (1964), 49–53.

69

Karasek, Hellmuth. "Fuer ein Theater, das sich nicht begnuegt," *Theater heute,* VII, xii (1966), 7–8.

K-d. "Hass und vulgaere Oede," *Generalanzeiger Ludwigshafen,* June 2, 1966.

Kessler, Sinah. "Auslands-Impressionen: Die italienische Spielzeit," *Theater heute,* V, vii (1964), 26–28.

kh. "Gebannt vom graesslich-grossartigen Stueck," *Westfaelische Rundschau* (Muenster), December 14, 1964.

k-h. "Moralische Anstalt oder Beduerfnisanstalt?" *Rhein-Neckar-Zeitung* (Heidelberg), June 29, 1966.

Kiaulehn, Walther. "Meine Angst vor Virginia Woolf," *Muenchner Merkur,* October 24, 1963.

Klose, G. Johannes. "Die Liebe—unsere schmerzlichste Erfahrung," *Duesseldorfer Schauspielhaus,* Programmheft 7 (1964/1965), enclosure.

Kraemer, Hermann-Josef. "Berliner Theaterwoche in Bad Godesberg: Albees Seelen-Strip-tease auf der Theaterbuehne," *Generalanzeiger fuer Bonn,* December 9, 1963.

Krebs-Goertz, Frances. "Wer hat Angst vor Virginia Woolf?" *Suedschleswigsche Heimatzeitung* (Flensburg), December 1, 1964.

Lau, Dieter. "Ein Kaufmann fuerchtet Virginia Woolf," *Sueddeutsche Zeitung* (Muenchen), October 12, 1965.

Lietzmann, Sabina. "Neuenglische Walpurgisnacht," *Komoedien-Werkstatt* (Basel), Programmheft 5 (1962/1963).
Appeared originally in the *Frankfurter Allgemeine Zeitung.*

Luft, Friedrich. "Deutsche Pressestimmen zu 'Wer hat Angst vor Virginia Woolf?' " *Pfalztheater*

Kaiserslautern, Programmheft. Appeared originally in *Die Welt* (Berlin).

Maass, Max Peter. "Edward Albee und die Komoedie des Todes," *Darmstaedter Tagblatt,* October 30, 1964.

Mayer, Adolf Suso. "Ein hoellisches Nocturno," *Rheinische Post* (Krefeld), April 10, 1967.

———."Im Duesseldorfer Schauspielhaus: Walpurgisnacht der Ehe," *Duisburger General-Anzeiger,* April 5, 1965.

Meier, Peter. "Einsamkeit zu zweit," *Stadttheater Bern,* Programmheft 4 (1965/1966).

Melchinger, Siegfried. "Erfundene oder beglaubigte Fabel," *Theater 1966 Chronik und Bilanz eines Buehnenjahres,* special yearly issue of *Theater heute,* August 20, 1966, 80–82.

———."Plaedoyer fuer den ungewoehnlichen Einzelnen," *Theater heute,* VI, x (1965), 5–8.

Mersmann, Heinrich. "Gastspiel in Braunschweig: Harter Dialog auf der Buehne," *Braunschweiger Zeitung,* May 16, 1966.

Meyer, A., Dr. "Schaubuehne und Hoerdrama," *Main-Post* (Wuerzburg), March 20, 1965.

Michaelis, Rolf. "Albees Spiel in den Tod," *Theater heute,* V, vi (1964), 12–13, 16–17, 20.

———."Fuer und wider 'Virginia Woolf,' " *Kammerspiele* (Muenchen), Programmheft 2 (1963/1964).

———."Spiel auf Tod und Leben," *Stuttgarter Zeitung,* January 9, 1964.

———."Toedliche Spiele," *Staedtische Buehnen* (Frankfurt am Main), Programmheft 11 (1964/1965).

Moschner, Manfred. "Das war ein amerikanischer Alptraum," *Koelnische Rundschau,* May 29, 1965.

Mudrich, Heinz. "Gesellschaftsspiele—einmal quer durch

die Hoelle," *Saarbruecker Zeitung,* May 10, 1965.

Nagel, Ivan. "Requiem fuer die Seele," *Die Neue Rundschau,* Heft 4 (1963), 646–651; *Kammerspiele* (Muenchen), Programmheft 2 (1963/1964).

Neumann, Joachim. "Die Anatomic einer 'modernen' Ehe," *Hamburger Echo am Abend,* April 13, 1964.

"Notizen: Auslandsrundblick." *Theater heute,* VI, iv (1965), 42–45.

Obzyna, G. "Mittwoch in der Josefstadt: 'Wer hat Angst vor Virginia Woolf . . .?' Eheschlamm-Badekur fuer Nichtabonnenten," *Express* (Wien), April 17, 1964.

P. D. "Quaelerei im Quartett," *Die Welt* (Hamburg), November 16, 1966.

Petersen, Hilde. "Furioso des Geschlechterhasses," *Rhein-Neckar-Zeitung* (Heidelberg), October 22, 1964.

Plagemann, Bernd. "Buehnen der Hansestadt Luebeck: Nahkampf-Theater," *Luebecker Morgen,* November 11, 1966.

R. H. " 'Virginia Woolf' ist zu verkraften," *Hildesheimer Rundschau,* October 13, 1966.

Range, Manfred. "Catch-as-catch-can im Theater," *Tagesanzeiger* (Regensburg), September 26, 1966.

Richter, Siegbert. " 'Wer hat Angst vor Virginia Woolf?' " *Luebecker Nachrichten,* April 14, 1964.

Richter, Wolfgang. "Kammerspiele Aachen: Die Nacht der nackten Wahrheit," *Aachener Volkszeitung,* September 29, 1964.

Rischbieter, Henning. "Wohin gehen die Berliner Festwochen?" *Theater heute,* IV, xi (1963), 12, 18.

Rismondo, Piero. "Abgesang vor Anbruch der Ameisenwelt," *Die Presse* (Wien), April 17, 1964.

Roth, Moritz. "Wer hat Angst vor Edward Albee?"

Secondary Sources

Badische Allgemeine Zeitung (Karlsruhe), July 1,
1964.

Salmony, George. "Gesang ueber Abwaessern,"
Abendzeitung (Muenchen), October 24, 1963.

Schlocker, Georges. "In Paris und um Paris," *Theater
heute,* VI, iii (1965), 38–41.

Schmidt, Dietmar N. "Kritische Chronik: Regensburg,"
Theater heute, VIII, i (1967), 57–58.

Schmidt, Hannes, Dr. "Nicht allein sein koennen,"
Wuppertaler Buehnen, Programmheft 25 (1964/1965).
"Die Party in der Hoelle," *Neue Rhein-Zeitung*
(Koeln), May 29, 1965.
"Das Skelett einer Hassliebe," *Neue Rhein-Zeitung*
(Duesseldorf), April 5, 1965.

Schroeder, Walter. "Party auf einem Vulkan," *Bild-
Zeitung* (Hamburg), April 14, 1964.

Schulz-Seitz, Ruth Eva. *Edward Albee— der Dichterphilosoph der Buehne.* Frankfurt am Main:
Vittorio Klostermann, 1966.

se. " 'Virginia Woolf' in Freiburg," *Stuttgarter Nachrichten,*
October 18, 1966.

Simon, John. "Am Broadway und off Broadway," *Theater
heute,* IV, iii (1963), 24–29.
American critic.

Smith, Norman. "Bevor die Uhr Mitternacht schlaegt,"
Freie Presse (Bielefeld), February 9, 1963.

Stein, Walter. "Viel Alkohol," *Rhein- Neckar-Zeitung*
(Heidelberg), May 31, 1966.

Sussdorff, Angela. "Edward Albee 'Wer hat Angst vor
Virginia Woolf,' " *Oldenburgisches Staatstheater,*
Programmheft 22 (1966/1967).

Tallert, Harry. "Albee: 'Wer hat Angst vor Virginia Woolf?'

Ehehoelle— Whiskyhoelle— Selbsthoelle,"
Bremerhavener Buergerzeitung, March 27, 1965.

Th. T. "Stuecke von O'Neill und Albee in Zuerich,"
Stuttgarter Zeitung, April 1, 1964.

"Theater-Premiere am Freitag, dem 13. November."
Die Welt (Berlin), November 11, 1964.

"Theaternachrichten." *Wuerttembergische Staatstheater
Stuttgart,* Programmheft 5 (1963/1964).

Thiem, Willy H. "Albee-Premiere in Muenchen: Haben alle
Angst vor Virginia Woolf?" *Abendpost* (Frankfurt am
Main), November 7, 1963.

——"Zum Titel," *Studio Stadttheater Hildesheim,*
Programmheft (1965/1966).

Torberg, Friedrich. " 'Virginia Woolf' Schlosspark-Theater
Berlin," *Theater 1964 Chronik und Bilanz eines
Buehnenjahres,* special yearly issue of *Theater heute,*
August 20, 1964, 40–41.

Trauthig, H.A. "Hinrichtung einer Ehe," *Elmshorner
Nachrichten,* April 16, 1964.

-tz. "Keine Angst vor Virginia Woolf," *Kieler Nachrichten,*
November 30, 1964.

uhl. "Abonnenten," *Die Welt* (Hamburg), October 13,
1965.

"Um die 'guten Sitten.' " *Hamburger Morgenpost,* October
13, 1965.

Vielhaber, Gerd. "Albees Hoellenparty," *Frankfurter
Rundschau,* April 10, 1965.

——"Deutsche Pressestimmen zu 'Wer hat Angst vor
Virginia Woolf?' " *Pfalztheater Kaiserslautern,*
Programmheft.
Appeared originally in the *Rheinische Post*
(Duesseldorf).

Secondary Sources

W. "Wer hat Angst vor Virginia Woolf?" *Podium* (Regensburg), Programmheft (1966/1967).

W. W. "Kommentiert: Wer hat Angst?" *Westfaelische Nachrichten* (Muenster), April 22, 1964.

Wagner, Klaus. "Alptraum: Hamburger Premieren," *Frankfurter Allgemeine,* April 30, 1964.

Waidelich, Juergen-Dieter, Dr. "Hat Bremerhaven Angst vor Virginia Woolf?" *Nordsee-Zeitung* (Bremerhaven), March 24, 1965.

Weibel, Kurt. "Geliebtes Fegefeuer," *Stadttheater Bern,* Programmheft 4 (1965/1966).

"Wer hat Angst vor Virginia Woolf?" *d'Letzeburger Land* (Luxemburg), November 1, 1963.

"Wer hat Angst vor Virginia Woolf?" *Theater Bremen,* Programmheft (1964/1965).

Werkbuehne des Stadttheaters St. Gallen. Anon. review, Programmheft (1965/1966).

Westecker, Wilhelm. "Schlossparktheater in Berlin: Lebenstanz der Grausamkeit," *Christ und Welt* (Stuttgart), No. 43 (1963), 18.

wgi. "Mitten ins Herz," *Heidelberger Tageblatt,* October 25, 1963.

WH. "Test mit Albee," *Weser-Kurier* (Bremen), March 27, 1965.

Wild, Winfried. "Ein Totentanz unserer Moralbegriffe," *Stuttgarter Nachrichten,* January 9, 1964.

Wilken, Rolf. "Meine Themen stammen aus der Wirklichkeit," *Deutsches Schauspielhaus in Hamburg,* Programmheft 11 (1963/1964).

——."Zum Stueck," *Studio Stadttheater Hildesheim,* Programmheft (1965/1966).

Ziegler, Karl Kurt. "Mit abgekratzten Etiketten,"

Westfaelische Rundschau (Recklinghausen), April 5,
1965.

"Zu den Plaenen fuer die neue Spielzeit," *Theater heute,*
V, ix (1964), 47–48.

"Zu: 'Wer hat Angst vor Virginia Woolf.'" *Stadttheater*
Bremerhaven 1964/65, Programmheft 15.

"Zum 50. Male." *Telegraf* (Berlin), April 14, 1964.

"Zum Stueck." *Wuerttembergische Staatstheater. Kleines*
Haus (Stuttgart), Programmheft (1964).

"Zur Entstehung von 'Virginia Woolf.'" *Komoedie Basel,*
Programmheft 3 (1964/1965).

Zwischen Kognak und Whisky: Letzte Proben fuer 'Wer
hat Angst vor Virginia Woolf?' " *Hamburger*
Abendblatt, April 9, 1964.

The Ballad of the Sad Cafe

Berg, Robert von. "Eine Ballade vom traurigen Café,"
Sueddeutsche Zeitung (Muenchen), October 30,
1963.

——:"Die Ballade vom traurigen Café," *Die Tat*
(Zuerich), November 19, 1963.

Braun, Hanns. "Erstauffuehrung: Siegfried aus USA,"
Christ und Welt (Stuttgart), December 11, 1964.

Burger, Eric. "Das Roulettespiel Liebe," *Deutsche Zeitung*
mit Wirtschaftszeitung (Koeln), November 7, 1963.

Colberg, Klaus. " 'Die Ballade vom traurigen Café,'"
Mannheimer Morgen, December 4, 1964.

Danler, Karl-Robert. "Kammerspiele Muenchen. Edward
Albee: 'Die Ballade vom traurigen Café,'"
Saarbruecker Landeszeitung, December 9, 1964.

Drews, Wolfgang. "Der Western mit der Widerspenstigen,"

Frankfurter Allgemeine, December 7, 1964.

Ell, Erik G. "Albees neue 'Ballade' braucht einen Zwerg," *Abendpost* Ausg. D. (Frankfurt am Main), November 29, 1963.

——:"Drei Broadway-Erfolge: 'Der Regenmacher' in neuer Fassung/ Albees 'Ballade des traurigen Cafés' gut angekommen," *Wiesbadener Tagblatt,* December 18, 1963.

FR. "Das Drama der Riesin," *Spandauer Volksblatt* (Berlin), November 2, 1963.

George, Manfred. "Ein neues Werk von Edward Albee," *National-Zeitung* (Basel), November 13, 1963.

H. B. K. "Hitler haelt Hetzrenden am Broadway: New York sieht Brechts 'Arturo Ui' / Albee-Stueck nach Carson McCullers," *Weser-Kurier* (Bremen), November 16, 1963.

Jenny, Urs. "Die undramatisierte Novelle," *Theater heute,* VI, i (1965), 38.

——:"Verlorene Liebesmueh," *Der Tagesspiegel* (Berlin), December 10, 1964.

Kaiser, Joachim. "Schweikarts Wirklichkeit—McCullers' Wahrheit," *Sueddeutsche Zeitung* (Muenchen), December 4, 1964.

Katz, Annerose. "Premiere: Der brave Ehemann haelt es mit den Faeusten," *Frankfurter Nachtausgabe,* December 11, 1964.

Kiaulehn, Walther. "Kammerspiel-Premiere: Edward Albees 'Ballade vom traurigen Café.' Die Riesendame und ihr Zwerg," *Muenchner Merkur,* December 4, 1964.

Kranz, H.B. "Das dunkle Mysterium der Liebe," *Mannheimer Morgen,* November 7, 1963.

—."Der fabelhafte Invalide: Broadway zwischen den Spielzeiten — 30 Neuheiten mit Skepsis," *Stuttgarter Nachrichten,* August 19, 1963.

kth. "Heute Albee-Premiere in den Kammerspielen: Miss Amelias Maenner," *Abendzeitung* (Muenchen), December 2, 1964.

Kuhner, Ingelore. "Wenn die Wimmer catcht . . .," *Frankfurter Neue Presse,* December 10, 1964.

Lehmann, H. "Der neue 'Albee,' " *Wiesbadener Kurier,* December 4, 1964.

Lietzmann, Sabina. "Ballade vom traurigen Café," *Frankfurter Allgemeine,* November 2, 1963.

Mokrau, A.K. " 'Ballade vom traurigen Café, " *Die Andere Zeitung* (Hamburg), December 17, 1964.

"Neues Stueck Albees uraufgefuehrt: "Die Ballade des traurigen Cafés,' " anon. review of the New York opening, *Luebecker Nachrichten,* November 1, 1963.

Ornstein, Lo. "Die Ballade vom traurigen Café," *Muenchner Merkur,* December 2, 1964.

Petzet, Wolfgang. "Penthesilea der Suedstaaten." *Badische Zeitung* (Freiburg), December 5, 1964.

Rainer, Wolfgang. "Puritanische Tragoedie," *Stuttgarter Zeitung,* December 4, 1964,

Reifferscheidt, Helly M. "Muenchener Theater," *Die Weltbuehne,* 52 (1964), 1655–1658.

Rode, Heinz. "Die Ballade vom traurigen Kaffee," *Nuernberger Nachrichten,* December 4, 1964.

Sahl, Hans. "Die Ballade vom traurigen Café," *Neue Zuercher Zeitung,* November 14, 1963.

——."Penthesilea in Blue jeans und Gummistiefeln," *Die Welt* (Berlin), November 12, 1963.

Seidenfaden, Ingrid. "Albee ohne Giftzaehne,"

Secondary Sources

Handelsblatt (Duesseldorf), December 4, 1964.

Stauch-von Quitzow, Wolfgang. "Penthesilea aus den Suedstaaten," *Westfaelische Rundschau* (Dortmund), December 8, 1964.

Sueskind, W.E. "Albee auf wildromantisch," *Frankfurter Rundschau,* December 7, 1964.

Wild, Winfried. "Edward Albee schreibt poetisch-episches Theater," *Schwaebische Zeitung* (Leutkirch), December 5, 1964.

"Zu den Plaenen fuer die neue Spielzeit." *Theater heute,* V, ix (1964), 47–48.

Tiny Alice

"Albee: Schloss im Schloss." *Der Spiegel,* No. 3 (1965), 68.

Althoff, Juergen. "Verwirrend, hoechst verwirrend," *Schwaebische Donau-Zeitung* (Ulm), February 8, 1966.

Beckmann, Heinz, "Alice —oder der dreizehnte Psalm," *Rheinischer Merkur* (Koblenz), February 11, 1966.

Berg, Robert von. "Ein Abend der Taeuschungen," *Handelsblatt* (Duesseldorf), January 15, 1965.

——"Mutmassungen ueber Julian," *Sueddeutsche Zeitung* (Muenchen), January 5, 1965.

——"Wer weiss, was soll das bedeuten?" *Sueddeutsche Zeitung* (Muenchen), April 23, 1965.

Berndt, Hans. "Zwischen Krimi und Mysterium," *Saarbruecker Zeitung,* February 11, 1966.

Breuer, Robert. "Faust unter der Duerrenmattscheibe," *Mannheimer Morgen,* January 18, 1965.

Brock-Sulzer, Elisabeth. "Religioese Erotik?" *Theater heute,* VII, vii (1966), 43–45.

Buetow, Hans. "Deutsche Albee-Erstauffuehrung: Wer ist
die Winzige Alice?" *Frankfurter Neue Presse,*
February 5, 1966.

Daiber, Hans. "Ein metaphysisches Traumspiel,"
Handelsblatt (Duesseldorf), February 7, 1966.

Drath, Viola Herms. "Theater am Broadway," *Madame,*
No. 4 (1965), 18.

ebs. "Fragwuerdige Wiederbegegnung mit Albee," *Die
Tat* (Zuerich), June 6, 1966.

Ferber, Christian. "Ein verfehltes Mysterium," *Die Welt*
(Berlin), February 5, 1966.

George, Manfred. "Etwas sehr Kleines," *Stuttgarter
Zeitung,* January 5, 1965.

——."Mutmassung um 'Tiny Alice,' " *Der Tagesspiegel*
(Berlin), April 8, 1965.

——."Von der Virginia Woolf zur reizenden Alice,"
Koelner Stadtanzeiger, January 7, 1965.

——."Zurueck zu den Ahnen," *Theater heute,* VI, ii
(1965), 15–17.

Gilles, Werner. "Edward Albees raetselhafter Schrei nach
Gott," *Mannheimer Morgen,* May 31, 1966.

Harmssen, Henning. "Alice aus dem All," *Vorwaerts*
(Bonn), February 16, 1966.

Heins, Carl. "Edward Albees 'Winzige Alice,'" *Die
Andere Zeitung* (Hamburg), February 10, 1966.

Herrmann, Walter M. "Deutsche Erstauffuehrung im
Schauspielhaus: Die Versuchungen des heiligen
Julian," *Hamburger Abendblatt,* February 4, 1966.

Herrmann, Wilhelm. "Albees 'Alice,'" *Weser-Kurier*
(Bremen), February 5, 1966.

Holz, Hans Heinz. "Albees 'Tiny Alice' im Zuercher
Schauspielhaus: Bildungsmystik—amerikanisch,"

National-Zeitung (Basel), June 14, 1966.

Ignee, Wolfgang. "Gott wird vermutet," *Christ und Welt* (Stuttgart), February 11, 1966.

Jacobi, Johannes. "Edward Albee gibt Raetsel auf," *Der Tagesspiegel* (Berlin), February 12, 1966.

———."Unser Kritiker sah: Winzige Alice," *Die Zeit* (Hamburg), February 11, 1966.

Jacobs, Wilhelm. "Ein Traumspiel?" *Frankfurter Rundschau,* February 7, 1966.

"Juni-Festwochen Zuerich 1966: "Winzige Alice.' " *Neue Zuercher Zeitung,* June 9, 1966.

Kaiser, Joachim. "Die beiden Dimensionen Albees," *Sueddeutsche Zeitung* (Muenchen), February 5, 1966.

———."Everdings Glueck mit Fraeulein Alice," *Sueddeutsche Zeitung* (Muenchen), June 20, 1966.

Karasek, Hellmuth. "Winzig," *Stuttgarter Zeitung,* February 7, 1966.

"Leckerbissen auf fremden Lippen." *Darmstaedter Echo,* July 5, 1966.

Lietzmann, Sabina. "Godot heisst hier Alice," *Frankfurter Allgemeine,* January 4, 1965.

Loon, Gerard Willem van. "Broadway: Albee spielt Picasso," *Die Buehne* (Wien), No. 78 (1965).

Neukirchen, Alfons. "Ein sehr frecher Reisser mit metaphysischer Sprengladung," *Westdeutsche Rundschau* (Wuppertal), February 5, 1966.

Peters, Karsten. "Everding inszeniert Albee in Zuerich: Pop aus der Schweiz," *8-Uhr-Blatt* (Nuernberg), June 7, 1966.

Rischbieter, Henning. "Chancen der Fiktion," *Theater 1966 Chronik un Bilanz eines Buehnenjahres,* special yearly issue of *Theater heute,* August 20, 1966, 82—83.

Sahl, Hans. "Passionsspiel oder Gangsterdrama?" *Die Welt* (Berlin), January 6, 1965.

Schaerer, Bruno. "Grosse Szenen in einem dubiosen Stueck," *Die Weltwoche* (Zuerich), June 10, 1966.

Schulz-Seitz, Ruth Eva. *Edward Albee —der Dichterphilosoph der Buehne.* Frankfurt am Main: Vittorio Klostermann, 1966.

Smith, Norman. "Albee beherrscht den Broadway," *Altenaer Kreisblatt,* July 1, 1965.

Textor, L.A. "Theater USA 1965," *d'Letzeburger Land* (Luxemburg), December 23, 1965.

Vielhaber, Gerd. " 'Metaphysisches Traumspiel' aus USA," *Neuss-Grevenbroicher Zeitung* (Neuss), February 5, 1966.

Wagner, Klaus. "Mysterienspiel von der Maus im Modell," *Frankfurter Allgemeine,* February 5, 1966.

Wendt, Ernst. "Alice 38," *Theater heute,* VII, iii (1966), 12–15.

Wiese, Eberhard von. "Menschen im Spiegelkabinett," *Hamburger Abendblatt,* January 8, 1966.

Wilken, Rolf. "Gedanken zu 'Winzige Alice,' " *Deutsches Schauspielhaus in Hamburg,* Programmheft 7 (1965/1966).

" 'Winzige Alice.' " *Neue Zuercher Zeitung,* June 9, 1966.

Malcolm

Berg, Robert von. "Spiel mit glaesernen Diamanten," *Sueddeutsche Zeitung,* (Muenchen), January 20, 1966.

Breuer, Robert. "Ein amerikanischer Parsifal," *Mannheimer Morgen,* January 20, 1966.

——"Mephisto und ein junger Parsifal," *Duesseldorfer*

Secondary Sources

Nachrichten, January 18, 1966.
Lietzmann, Sabina. "Kaspar Hauser im Prunkhotel,"
    Frankfurter Allgemeine, January 15, 1966.
Sahl, Hans. "Sehnsucht nach dem Vaterbild," *Die Welt*
    (Berlin), January 21, 1966.
SL. "Albee abgesetzt," *Frankfurter Allgemeine,* January
    22, 1966.

A Delicate Balance

"Albees 'Empfindliches Gleichgewicht' franzoesisiert."
    Theater heute, IX, ii (1968), 21.
"Akademietheater: 'Empfindliches Gleichgewicht' 'A
    delicate Balance'), ein grossartiger Schauspielerabend
    mit dem neuesten Stueck von Edward Albee." *Die*
    Buehne, Heft 105 (1967), 3.
Berg, Robert von. "Die Leere im Verhoer," *Sueddeutsche*
    Zeitung (Muenchen), September 27, 1966.
——"Eine seelische Vivisektion," *Handelsblatt*
    (Duesseldorf), September 28, 1966.
——"Whisky um halb neun," *Sonntagsblatt* (Hamburg),
    October 9, 1966.
Blaha, Paul. "Balanceakt eines Theaterabends. Samstag,
    Akademietheater: Albees 'Empfindliches Gleichge-
    wicht' mit Wessely, Muench," *Kurier* (Wien), May 2,
    1967.
Breuer, Robert. "Edward Albee gibt dem Broadway ein
    Zugstueck," *Westdeutsche Rundschau* (Wuppertal),
    September 29, 1966.
Buschkiel, Juergen. "Kritische Chronik: Basel," *Theater*
    heute, VIII, xii (1967), 52–53.
Claire. "Drinks," *Theater heute,* VIII, viii (1967), 43.

Dannenberg, Peter. "Deutsches Schauspielhaus Hamburg: Das Ereignis einer Schuh-Inszenierung, 'Empfindliches Gleichgewicht' von E. Albee," *Die Buehne,* Heft 109 (1967), 19.

Drath, Viola Herms. "Theater Off Broadway," *Madame,* No. 4 (1967), 26.

Drews, Wolfgang. "Die besagte Angst im Nacken: Albees 'Empfindliches Gleichgewicht' und Grass 'Plebejer' in Muenchen," *Frankfurter Allgemeine Zeitung,*, May 3, 1967.

——:"Wer hat Angst vor Edward Albee?: 'Empfindliches Gleichgewicht' — Deutsche Erstauffuehrung in Muenchen," *Tagesspiegel* (Berlin), May 6, 1967.

"Edward Albee: Prekaeres Gleichgewicht." Exerpts from reviews by Ingrid Seidenfaden, Klaus Goldberg, Urs Jenny (see Jenny), Hellmuth Karasek (see Karasek), Wolfgang Drews (see Drews), Walther Kiaulehn and Erich Pfeiffer-Belli (see Pfeiffer-Belli), *Volksbuehnenspiegel,* XIII, vii/viii (1967), 15.

F. R. " 'Empfindliches Gleichgewicht': Deutsche Erstauffuehrung in den Muenchner Kammerspielen," *Theater-Rundschau,* XIII, vi (1967), 2.

"Fuer ihr Publikum, gegen ihr Publikum —was spielen die deutschen Theater 1967/1968." *Theater 1967 Chronik und Bilanz eines Buehnenjahres,* special yearly issue of *Theater heute,* August 20, 1967, 5–22.

Haas, Willy, "Schwestern der Virginia Woolf: Albees 'Empfindliches Gleichgewicht' — Premiere im Schauspielhaus," *Die Welt* (Hamburg), September 11, 1967.

hib. "Ein Kartenhaus faellt zusammen: Beifall fuer Edward Albees 'Empfindliches Gleichgewicht' im Deutschen

Schauspielhaus," *Hamburger Abendblatt,* September
9, 1967.

Jacobi, Johannes. "Rituale zwischen Angst und Freund-
schaft. Unser Kritiker sah: Empfindliches Gleichgewicht, Stueck von Edward Albee, Muenchner
Kammerspiele, Wiener Burgtheater im Akademietheater," *Die Zeit* (Hamburg), May 12, 1967.

Kaiser, Joachim. "Notruf von der Donau: Wiener
Festwochen-Alltag," *Sueddeutsche Zeitung*
(Muenchen), May 26, 1967.

Karasek, Hellmuth. "Erstauffuehrung an den Muenchner
Kammerspielen: Der Fall Albees, 'Empfindliches
Gleichgewicht,' " *Stuttgarter Zeitung,* April 28,
1967.

Karsch, Walther. "Gleichgewicht leicht gestoert: Oscar
Fritz Schuh inszenierte Edward Albee," *Tagesspiegel*
(Berlin), September 10, 1967.

"Komoedie Basel: Albees 'Empfindliches Gleichgewicht.' "
Die Buehne, Heft 112 (1968), 24.

Lietzmann, Sabina. "Verzweiflung im Salon," *Frankfurter
Allgemeine,* September 28, 1966.

Michaelis, Rolf. "Edward Albee wiederholt sich," *Theater
heute,* VIII, vi (1967), 16–21.

——:"Schauspieler-Stuecke?" *Theater 1967 Chronik
und Bilanz eines Buehnenjahres,* special yearly issue
of *Theater heute,* August 20, 1967, 107.

Nagel, Ivan. "Besitz oder Gemeinschaft: Ueber Albees
'Empfindliches Gleichgewicht,' " *Kammerspiele*
(Muenchen), Programmheft 6 (1966/1967)
Programmheft 9 (1967/1968).

Nennecke, Charlotte. "Die ansteckende Angst,"
Sueddeutsche Zeitung (Muenchen), April 26, 1967.

"Der neue Albee: 'Delikate Balance.' " *Der Kurier* (Berlin), September 28, 1966.

Penzoldt, Guenther. "Es sind doch unsere besten Freunde!" *Deutsches Schauspielhaus Hamburg,* Programmheft 1 (1967/1968).

Pfeiffer-Belli, Erich. "Amerikanische Oednis: Albees Schauspiel 'Empfindliches Gleichgewicht' — Premiere in Muenchen," *Die Welt,* April 28, 1967.

Pollak, Paul. "Nacht mit Gaesten," *Twen,* April 1967.

Sahl, Hans. "Die Welt besteht nicht aus Maertyrern," *Die Welt* (Berlin), September 28, 1966.

Schlocker, Georges. "Pariser Brueche," *Theater heute,* IX, ii (1968), 21.

Urs, Jenny. "Arien an der Hausbar: Albees 'Empfindliches Gleichgewicht' in den Muenchner Kammerspielen," *Sueddeutsche Zeitung* (Muenchen), April 4, 1967.

Wilk, Gerard H. "Kein Sohn von Virginia Woolf," *Der Tagesspiegel* (Berlin), October 5, 1966.

Everything in the Garden

Beradt, Charlotte. "Bericht vom Broadway," *Theater heute,* IX, iv (1968), 39–40.

Berg, Robert von. "Finanzierungsprobleme in Suburbia: Edward Albees Version von 'Everything in the Garden' in New York uraufgefuehrt," *Sueddeutsche Zeitung* (Muenchen), December 7, 1967.

Ell, Erik G. "Umstrittene Albee-Premiere in New York: Eine bittere, zynische, aber faszinierende Komedie. Ehekrach in einer bruechigen Welt," *Hamburger Abendblatt,* December 9, 1967.

Honegger, Gitta. "Die Gattinen, die teuren. Ein neuer

Secondary Sources

Albee am Broadway: 'Everything in the Garden,' "
Stuttgarter Zeitung, December 14, 1967.
Leitzmann, Sabina. "Albee mit Zeigefinger: Urauffuehrung
am Broadway," *Frankfurter Allgemeine Zeitung,*
December 18, 1967.
Sahl, Hans. "Strychnin fuer Konformisten: Albees neues
Stueck 'Alles in den Garten' —Premiere in New
York," *Die Welt,* December 7, 1967.

Box—Mao—Box

Beradt, Charlotte. "Bericht vom Broadway," *Theater
heute,* IX, iv (1968), 39—40.
Berg, Robert von. "Der neue Albee im Schatten Becketts?
'Box-Mao-Box' in einem Werkraumtheater Buffalos
uraufgefuehrt," *Sueddeutsche Zeitung* (Muenchen),
April 6, 1968.

Other Countries

Primary Sources

(Arranged chronologically)

PLAYS

Czechoslovakia

Balada o smutné Kavárně. Luba and Rudolf Pellar. Praha:
Dilia, 1964.
Hry. Milan Lukăs. Praha: Orbis, 1964.
Kdo se bojí Virginie Woolfové. (Kdo by se Kafky bal).
Luba and Rudolf Pellar. Praha: Dilia, 1964.
Stalo se v zoo. Wanda Zámecká. Praha: Dilia, 1964.
Smrt Bessie Smithové. Bedřich Becher. Praha: Dilia, 1965.

Denmark

Hvem er bange for Virginia Woolf? Asta Hoff Jørgensen.
København: Gyldendal, 1964.
Zoo Story. John Hahn-Petersen and Preben Harris.
København: Gyldendal, 1966.

France

Qui a peur de Virginia Woolf? Jean Cau. Paris: Laffont,
1964.
"Qui a peur de Virginia Woolf?" Jean Cau. *L'Avant-Scène,*
CCCXXXIX (August 1965), 10–51.
*Le rêve de l'Amérique. Zoo story. La mort de Bessie
Smith. Le tas de sable.* George Belmont and Elisabeth
Janvier. Paris: Laffont, 1965.

91

Zoo Story. Matthieu Galey. *L'Avant-Scène,* CCCXXXIV
(May 1965), 9–16.

Délicate balance. Paris: Laffont, 1968

Italy

Chi ha paura di Virginia Woolf? Ettore Capriolo. Milano:
Bompiani, 1963.

Nuovo teatro americano: La morte di Bessie Smith, et al.
Furio Colombo. Milano: Bompiani, 1963.

Il sogno americano e altre commedie. Ettore Capriolo.
Milano: Bompiani, 1963.

Netherlands

*Het verhaal van de dierentuin. De dood van Bessie Smith.
De droom van Amerika.* Gerard Kornelis van het
Reve. Amsterdam: Van Ditmar, 1964.

Wie is er bang voor Virginia Woolf? Gerard Kornelis van
het Reve. Amsterdam: Van Ditmar, 1964 (1st
through 4th printing), 1965 (5th printing).

Het verhaal van de dierentuin. Gerard Kornelis van het
Reve. Amsterdam: Corvey, 1965.

Kleine Alice. Ernst van Altena. Amsterdam: Van Ditmar,
1965.

Norway

Hvem er redd for Virginia Woolf? Peter Magnus. Oslo:
Gyldendal, 1964.

Sweden

Vem aer raedd foer Virginia Woolf? Oesten Sjoestrand.
Stockholm: Bonniers, 1964.

Secondary Sources
(Arranged alphabetically)

France

L'Avant-Scène. CCCXXXIV (May 1965), 7.
Production information and cast for *The Zoo Story* in Paris.

L'Avant-Scène. CCCXXXIX (August 1965), 7.
Production information and cast for *Who's afraid of Virginia Woolf* in Paris.

Cau, Jean. "Edward Albee: Une bombe!" *L'Avant-Scène,* CCCXXXIX (August 1965), 9.

"La Critique: Qui A Peur De Virginia Woolf?" *L'Avant-Scène,* CCCXXXIX (August 1965), 52. Parts of eight reviews.

"La Critique: Zoo Story." *L'Avant-Scène,* CCCXXXIV (May 1965), 17. Parts of seven reviews.

Dommergues, Pierre. "Le théatre américain de l'absurde," *Lettres Nouvelles,* XIII (March-April 1965), 148–160.

Galey, Matthieu. "Albee sur le chemin de la gloire," *Nouvelles Littéraires,* No. 1954, XLIII (February 11, 1965), 13.

——."Un Auteur Modeste," *L'Avant-Scène,* CCCXXXIV (May 1965), 6.

Mignon, Paul-Louis. "Le théatre de A Jusqu'à Z," *L'Avant-Scène,* CCCXXXIX (August 1965), 8.

Sauvage, Leo. "Les américains auraient-ils peur d'Edward Albee?" *Figaro Littéraire,* No. 1034 (1966).

Edward Albee At Home And Abroad

Hungary

Hankiss, Elemér. "Who's Afraid of Edward Albee?" *The New Hungarian Quarterly,* V, xv (1964), 168–174.

Italy

Corono, Mario. "Edward Albee," *Studi Americani,* X (1964), 369–394.

Guerrieri, Gerardo. "Dal diario di un traduttore," *Sipario,* I (November 1963).

Latin America

Rocha Filho, Rubem. "Albee: Processo e tentativa," *Tempo Brasileiro,* No. 3 (1963), 161–172.

Netherlands

Stroman, Ben. "Edward Albee's *Who's Afraid of Virginia Woolf?" De Vlaamse Gids,* XLVIII (1964), 342–344.

Poland

K., J. "Le dramaturge Américain Edward Albee à Varsovie." *Le Theâtre en Pologne.* Monthly bulletin of the Polish center of the International Theatre Institute. (February 1964), 19. English trans. on p. 25. Describes Albee's tour of Russia and satellite nations.

Przybylska, Krystyna. "Amerykański nurt awangardy," *Dialog,* 1962.

Secondary Sources

Sweden

Schein, Harry. "Vem aer raedd foer Virginia Woolf?"
  Bonniers Litteraera Magasin, XXX (1961),
  706–710.